Discovering the Treasures of God's Written Word

VOLUME FIVE

THE BOOK OF ACTS

Printed by Concept Marketing Inc.

Published by Crossroads Christian Communications Inc.
P.O. Box 5100, Burlington, Ontario L7R 4M2

ISBN 0-921702-95-7

"Nothing is so strong

as gentleness,

and nothing is so gentle

as real strength."

~ De Sales

This book is lovingly dedicated

to the One who set the standard

for strength in leadership,

the Saviour, Jesus.

And to the one who resembles Him

more than anyone I know,

my husband Ron.

Acknowledgments

A couple of years ago at a Christmas banquet, a new acquaintance innocently asked me, "So, who writes your material for you?" I have to be honest and tell you that my initial reaction was to want to point out, in no uncertain terms, *I write my own material, thank you very much!* But then that still small voice, that I have grown to love, whispered to me my answer. With a gracious smile (that honestly was not there seconds earlier) I said, "Actually, I do have a Co-author — God's Holy Spirit. Without Him, nothing I come up with is any good!" I, more than anyone, know how true that is.

However, in this "collaboration", God has also brought along several "polishers" to aid in the process. While their official title may be "editor" or "proofreader", I prefer to think of them as those boundlessly talented and ever patient individuals who take text that was originally written for television, and *spiffy it up* with proper grammar and punctuation.

To *Karen Stowell* who worked closely with me on the first four books in this series – thank you for caring so much about the details!

To *Daina Doucett* – I will never see red ink again and not think of you! Thank you for making sure I followed the proper grammatical rules. And especially thank you for not minding when I broke a few!

And to the newest member of the team, *Michael Moon*
– thank you, Michael, for the endless hours you poured over this manuscript to make sure it was not only *very proper* – but also *very me.*

Introduction

God's Word is a never-ending "Treasure Chest" of divine wisdom, supernatural love, and even unexpected humour. Every time I open its cover, I discover another gem of truth to apply to my life.

It is my prayer that as we discover these gems together, we will feel challenged, cherished, and most of all, changed.

As we journey through God's "Love Letter" to mankind in this, the fifth volume of my *Sincerely Yours* series, may we continue to read it slowly, examine it closely, and discover the many "jewels" that make up the treasure that is God's Word.

Ann

Contents

Contents

A Book of Power

READ ACTS 1:1-11

The book of Acts was written by Luke, a Greek, a doctor, and a very close friend of the apostle Paul. Luke also authored the Gospel of Luke, which is a historical account of the birth, life, death, and resurrection of Jesus. Acts, however, is known primarily as the history book of the early Church. Unlike the four Gospels, Acts is not named after a person, but rather after a course of events. Most agree it details the Acts of the apostles. However, to be a little more precise, perhaps we should clarify to say that it actually records the Acts of the Holy Spirit *through* the apostles. From the very first passage we find that the Holy Spirit of God, not any mortal man, is the main character of the book of Acts, and He was given by the resurrected Jesus. Reading in verse eight, let's hear the words of Jesus to His disciples as He describes just some of what they could expect.

> *"But when the Holy Spirit has come upon you, you will receive power and will tell people about Me everywhere – in Jerusalem, throughout Judea, in Samaria, and to the ends of the earth"* (Acts 1:8).

When you receive the Holy Spirit, you will receive power. But, what kind of power? I like the way the commentator put it in the introduction to Acts in the *New Living Translation* of the Bible. He compares our spiritual life to a flashlight. "The switch on the flashlight clicks" he says, "but instead of a bright beam piercing the darkness, there is only a faint yellow glow. The batteries are weak and low; there is not much power left." Sounds a lot like us.

We want to shine brightly for God, but in our own power, the best we can manage is a dull flicker. We need an external power source – we need to be filled with God's Holy Spirit. And that is the gist of the book of Acts – ordinary people doing extraordinary things because of their surrender to God's incredible power. It records the birth and growth of the Christian Church from the seed of the Holy Spirit.

When you receive the Holy Spirit, you will receive power.

And so, the book of Acts is a book of power. It is the power given through God's Holy Spirit to take the truth of Jesus to a lost world. It is the power to supply us with the ability for living a successful and fulfilling life for God, and the source that will carry us through life's hardest trials that are sure to come. In short, as one author put it, the book of Acts "is the powerhouse for believers."

A Gift of Promise

READ ACTS 1:12-26

Christmastime! For many it's a time of food, fun, and family. But for some, because of life's circumstances, Christmas is anything but merry.

Dr. James Dobson tells a story of an elderly woman named Mrs. Thornhope who was struggling with her first Christmas alone. Her husband had died just a few months earlier from a slowly-developing cancer. Now, several days before Christmas, blizzard-like conditions left her snowed in, adding to her blanket of solitude.

Late one afternoon, after the snow had stopped falling, the doorbell rang and there stood a delivery boy with a box. He said, "Mrs. Thornhope?" She nodded. "Would you sign here, please?" he asked.

After inviting him in out of the cold, she signed the paper. "What's in the box?" she asked.

The young man laughed and opened the flap exposing a beautiful little golden retriever puppy. The boy picked up the squirming puppy and said, "He's for you, Ma'am. He's six weeks old and completely paper trained."

Well, Mrs. Thornhope was confused to say the least. "Who sent him?" she asked. The young man set down the puppy and handed her an envelope. "It's all explained in here, Ma'am," he said. "The dog was bought last July while its mother was still pregnant. It was meant to be a Christmas gift for you." He then handed her a book entitled, *How to Care for your Golden Retriever*.

In desperation, she asked again, "But who sent me this puppy?" As the young man turned to leave, he said, "Your husband, Ma'am. Merry Christmas."

Carrying her new puppy and her cherished letter to the sofa, Mrs. Thornhope began to read. Her husband had written the letter three weeks before he died and left it with the kennel owners to be delivered with the puppy as his last Christmas gift to her. His letter spoke of love and encouraged her to be strong. He said that he was waiting for that glorious day when she would join him, but that this loving dog would keep her company until then. A lonely Christmas was suddenly transformed by a gift of "hope." This reminds me of another gift – one the disciples of Jesus were told to expect.

Looking at Acts 1:12 - 26, the disciples of Jesus had just witnessed Him "being taken up into the sky." In verse 11, after they had said good-bye to their Friend, two "white-robed men suddenly stood there among them." They said:

> *"Men of Galilee, why are you standing here staring at the sky? Jesus has been taken away from you into Heaven. And someday, just as you saw Him go, He will return!"* (Acts 1:11).

What a glorious promise! In today's passage, we find Jesus' disciples gathered together in expectation of another promise – the arrival of the promised Holy Spirit. John chapter 14 records Jesus telling them that this precious Gift would arrive after He had gone. And now that He was gone, what did His disciples do?

> *"They all met together continually for prayer, along with Mary the mother of Jesus, several other women, and the brothers of Jesus"* (Acts 1:14).

They all met together continually for prayer! Jesus had given them a promise and they weren't about to take that promise lightly. Better than a warm puppy, the warmth of the promised Holy Spirit would provide comfort, confidence and courage, not just for a season, but for whatever their lives would face.

What about us? Has Jesus given us any promises? God's Word is full of His promises. Dig into your Bible! Grab onto those promises, and know the Hope that was born that very first Christmas.

The Power of His Presence

READ ACTS 2:1-13

During the depression, there was a certain sheep ranch owned by a man named Yates. Times were tough for the Yates family as the ranching business wasn't even enough to pay the principal and interest on their mortgage. They were in danger of losing their ranch. With little money for clothes or food, this family (like many others) had to live on government assistance. Day after day as he grazed his sheep on those rolling west Texas hills, Mr. Yates, the leader of the family, was no doubt troubled about how to pay his bills.

Then a seismographic crew from an oil company came into the area. They told him there might be oil on his land. He signed a contract granting them permission to drill a wildcat well, and was flabbergasted when, at 1,115 feet, they struck a huge oil reserve. The first well came in at 80,000 barrels a day. Many subsequent wells were more than twice as large. In fact, 30 years after the discovery a government test of one of the wells showed it still had the potential flow of 125,000 barrels of oil a day. And Mr. Yates owned it all. When he purchased the land, he owned the oil as well. A multimillionaire initially living in poverty. The problem? He didn't know the oil was there – even though he owned it.

This story was told by Dr. Bill Bright, founder of Campus Crusade for Christ. He noted that unknowingly many Christians live in spiritual poverty even though they can rightfully tap the wells of God's riches. We are entitled to the energizing power of God's Holy Spirit, but we live without Him – unaware. Here's what God's Word says about the gift of the Holy Spirit:

> *"On the day of Pentecost, seven weeks after Jesus' resurrection, the believers were meeting together in one place. Suddenly, there was a sound from Heaven like*

> *the roaring of a mighty windstorm in the skies above them, and it filled the house where they were meeting. Then what looked like flames or tongues of fire appeared and settled on each of them. And everyone present was filled with the Holy Spirit and began speaking in other languages, as the Holy Spirit gave them this ability"* (Acts 2:1-4).

The arrival of God's Holy Spirit was a powerful moment and the disciples were right in the middle of it. There was no mistaking His Presence. The wind blew mightily – the Spirit's Presence could be felt. The fire hovered above them – His Presence could be seen. And the gift of "tongues" was spoken – His Presence could be heard. God's Holy Spirit was among them; that was made perfectly clear. The disciples of Jesus were "*filled*" with Him – and we can be too.

No matter what our denomination, once we've been bought with the Blood of Jesus, we're to expect the arrival of the Holy Spirit. Don't live in spiritual poverty. Dig deeper into the things of God. Allow His Holy Spirit to overflow in your life. When you do, you'll be amazed at the very real evidence of His Holy Presence.

> *Many Christians live in 'spiritual' poverty. We are entitled to the energizing power of God's Holy Spirit, but we live without Him – unaware.*

Forever in His Arms

READ ACTS 2:14-36

Not long ago, I was privileged to have a story published in one of the *Chicken Soup For The Soul* books. The story was of the time we almost lost our two-and-a-half-year-old son in a swimming pool. Through a series of what some would call "coincidences," but we know to be "God-incidences," my husband Ron discovered our little son fighting for his life under the solar blanket in the frigid waters of the just-filled pool. I witnessed the whole thing from the kitchen window and re-lived it many times in my dreams.

But, as you can imagine, I wasn't the only one who had trouble coming to terms with what happened. For weeks afterward our son Eric woke up with nightmares about being surrounded by "blue bubbles." When we talked about the pool incident, Eric always explained it saying that "Jesus and Daddy saved me." But he still had the nightmares. That is until one day when my husband Ron came up with an idea.

In his unskilled artistic way Ron drew a picture of himself as he looked then, mustache and all, holding in his arms two-year-old Eric. But that wasn't all he drew. Standing behind Ron, in full beard and flowing robes, was Jesus, and He was holding in His arms both Eric and Eric's Daddy. We gave this picture to Eric and he taped it on his wall next to his pillow. We told him the next time he woke up with the nightmares, all he had to do was look at the picture and remember that he was never alone. Not long after that, Eric's nightmares about bubbles stopped.

God is always there. Sometimes we all need to be reminded of that truth. And in today's reading we will see that the apostle Peter, under the inspiration of God's Holy Spirit, did just that.

The Holy Spirit had just arrived in a very evident and powerful way. Because of this, a crowd primarily of Jews had gathered and "stood amazed and perplexed." *What's going on?* they wondered. To this crowd Peter preached his first sermon – marking that day as the birthday of the Church. The apostle Peter, full of God's Spirit, took centre stage – and shone the spotlight on Jesus.

> *"People of Israel, listen! God publicly endorsed Jesus of Nazareth by doing wonderful miracles, wonders, and signs through Him, as you well know. But you followed God's prearranged plan. With the help of lawless Gentiles, you nailed Him to the Cross and murdered Him. However, God released Him from the horrors of death and raised Him back to life again, for death could not keep Him in its grip"* (Acts 2:22-24).

In this, his first public sermon, Peter preached the resurrection of Jesus. His words were truth and hope. By personally applying them, his listeners received the promise of their own "resurrected" life. Quoting from Psalm 16, Peter emphasized hope in Jesus.

> *"King David said this about Him: 'I know the Lord is always with me. I will not be shaken, for He is right beside me. No wonder my heart is filled with joy, and my mouth shouts His praises! My body rests in hope'"* (Acts 2:25, 26).

My body rests in hope as well! The risen Jesus has conquered the grave. Because of Him, we need never be afraid. We can put our trust in Him. Whether you're 2 or 102, you can rest peacefully knowing that you are forever in His arms.

A Simple Message

READ ACTS 2:37-47

Ah ... the simple life! What comes to your mind when you hear that phrase? A peaceful and uncomplicated lifestyle? A life released from the competitiveness of our rat-race world? There's a lot to be said for simplifying our lives, getting back to basics, cutting out the excess. Freeing ourselves from the "unnecessary accumulation of things lying untidily about" – or as it's better known, *clutter.*

In our home "clutter" is a four-letter-word (okay, it's seven letters, but work with me). That's why for our family "big garbage day" is a time for celebration! Finally there's an occasion to throw away items like that ancient box refrigerator that looks like it was once owned by "Ozzie and Harriet." And the monstrous old box spring whose springs are now living "outside of the box." And of course there's the de-crepit de-humidifier that's been deceased longer than anyone can remember. Yes, once the clutter is gone, life takes on a whole new meaning – the glorious "simple life." It really is the only way to go. And as we will see in our reading, the apostle Peter, quite simply, believed the same thing.

Acts 2:37-47 is set in what is known as "The Day of Pentecost" – the day on time's calendar when the third Member of the Trinity, God's Holy Spirit, became personal with man.

The beginning of this chapter compares His arrival to that of a "roaring and mighty windstorm." As you can imagine, the obvious results of His Presence, caused quite a stir and produced quite a crowd. And that's when Peter stepped forward, probably recognized as a travelling companion of Jesus. But now Peter was full of the power and wisdom of God's Holy Spirit. I imagine that he could have spoken quite capably on any number of theological topics. His own personal understanding would have been so much clearer with the Presence of God's Spirit. So, what did Peter say to this large crowd?

> *"Each of you must turn from your sins and turn to God, and be baptized in the name of Jesus Christ for the forgiveness of your sins. Then you will receive the gift of the Holy Spirit"* (Acts 2:38).

Cutting out the clutter. Peter had the crowd's full attention, and what he chose to tell them was the simple message of the Cross.

Turn away from your sins. Turn to God. Why? Because of Jesus. It's as simple as that.

> *"The Day of Pentecost" - the day when the third Member of the Trinity, God's Holy Spirit, became personal with man.*

Heaven-Sent Wholeness

READ ACTS 3:1-11

The lost art of communication. Very few people these days can communicate clearly and concisely. William Penn, founder of the state of Pennsylvania, once said, "Be humble and gentle in your conversation; and of few words, but always pertinent when you speak." Augustine said, "Always beware of the man who abounds in eloquent nonsense." And then there's the old adage, "Never use a gallon of words to express a spoonful of thought."

Okay, maybe I should have stopped a few quarts ago – much like some high school writers of our day. An internet site records some actual attention-grabbing analogies found in high school papers:

"Her eyes were like two brown circles with big black dots in the centre."

"He spoke with the wisdom that can only come from experience like the guy who went blind because he looked at a solar eclipse without one of those boxes with a pinhole in it and now goes around the country speaking at high schools about the dangers of looking at a solar eclipse without one of those boxes with a pinhole in it."

"Her vocabulary was as bad as like whatever."

"Long separated by cruel fate, the star-crossed lovers raced across the grassy field toward each other like two freight trains, one having left Cleveland at 6:36 p.m. travelling at 55 mph and the other from Topeka at 4:19 p.m. at a speed of 35 mph."

"John and Mary had never met. They were like two hummingbirds who had also never met."

The lost art of communication! "Never use a gallon of words to express a spoonful of thought." Sometimes that's easier said than

done. But we see in Acts 3:1-11 that speaking clearly and concisely was something Peter did well.

We read that with the arrival of God's Holy Spirit, Jesus' disciples experienced an amazing anointing that enabled them to perform incredible miracles. The story of one such miracle begins with this passage:

> *"Peter and John went to the Temple one afternoon to take part in the three o'clock prayer service. As they approached the Temple, a man lame from birth was put beside the Temple gate so he could beg from the people going in"* (Acts 3:1, 2).

This man was a familiar beggar, kind of a fixture at the temple gate. Daily he sat at his post collecting from everyone either a spare coin or a quick glance. It's likely he spent most of his time in an absent-minded daze focussing more on the pockets than the faces of those from whom he begged. That's why, I believe, when he begged from Peter and John, they didn't respond the way he expected:

> *"Peter and John looked at him intently, and Peter said, 'Look at us!'"* (Acts 3:4).

This man wanted their money, but Peter wanted his attention. And he didn't mince words. Reminds me of when our children were younger and I'd try to explain something to them. Without fail, I'd begin my instructions with, "Look at my eyes." If I could get them to do that, I knew I had their attention. And so it was with Peter. He didn't want this man to beg and settle for man-made coins when he could give him heaven-sent wholeness. And we know the rest of the story. After accepting his healing, this renowned beggar *gave* all praise to God.

Short and sweet and to the point. Often that's the best way to convey the most important information. So, here goes: Jesus loves you. Let Him into your life. You'll be glad you did.

Where's the Baby?

READ ACTS 3:12-26

Through the power of God's Holy Spirit, Peter and John had just healed a well-known beggar who had sat at the Gate called Beautiful. Every day he had begged from people as they entered. When the news hit the street that he was suddenly healed and many had witnessed him walking and praising God, it spread like wildfire. In fact, in verse 11 we read,

> *"They all rushed out to Solomon's Colonnade, where he was holding tightly to Peter and John. Everyone stood there in awe of the wonderful thing that had happened"* (Acts 3:11).

God's power was amazing. Peter saw in the awe-struck crowd the perfect opportunity to give credit where credit was due.

> *"People of Israel,"* he said, *"what is so astounding about this? And why look at us as though we had made this man walk by our own power and godliness? For it is the God of Abraham, the God of Isaac, the God of Jacob, the God of all our ancestors who has brought glory to His Servant Jesus by doing this"* (Acts 3:12, 13a).

Instead of basking in the glow of people's admiration, Peter gave all the glory to God. And he did more. He narrowed the beam of his spotlight of praise:

> *"The name of Jesus has healed this man – and you know how lame he was before. Faith in Jesus' name has caused this healing before your very eyes"* (Acts 3:16).

Simple faith in the name of Jesus is what healed this man. Jesus deserves to be honoured. It's good to honour Jesus all year round, but especially when it's time to celebrate His birth.

Evangelist Luis Palau tells a story of a wealthy European family that decided to have their newborn baby baptized in their enormous mansion. Dozens of guests were invited to the elaborate affair. When they arrived they were all dressed in their best attire. After depositing their elegant wraps in an upstairs room, the guests gathered for first class entertainment. At the conclusion of the musical prelude, the time had come for the purpose of their gathering – the infant's baptismal ceremony. But where was the baby? No one seemed to know. The child's governess ran upstairs and soon returned with a desperate look on her face. Everyone searched frantically for the lost baby. Then someone recalled having seen him asleep on one of the beds. Indeed the baby *was* on a bed – buried beneath a pile of coats, jackets, and furs. The object of the day's celebration had been forgotten, neglected, and nearly smothered!

At Christmas, and throughout the year, let's make sure the Baby whose birthday we celebrate isn't hidden beneath the our traditions and materialism. Jesus is our focus. Let's approach every Christmas asking, "Where's the Baby?"

Jesus is our focus.

In the Presence of Jesus

READ ACTS 4:1-22

I don't know about your family, but our family definitely plays favourites – favourite movies, that is. From the pure silliness of Danny Kaye in *The Court Jester*, to the pure fantasy of the more recent *The Princess Bride*. We definitely have favourites. But you need to know that one of our all-time family favourites has to be the Peanuts Christmas classic, *A Charlie Brown Christmas*. In this animation, Charlie Brown and Linus are nominated to choose their class Christmas tree. One snowy night the two make their way through the tree-filled lot looking for the right one. That's when it happens.

Charlie Brown, who has always felt a little plain and un-spectacular, stumbles upon a tree that he can identify with. This Christmas tree is sad. While all the other trees are robust and full, this poor little specimen is homely and unpretentious. Certainly not the festive centre-piece the class had in mind. However, Charlie Brown doesn't see it that way. He makes the decision and they purchase the tree. But the kids at school are not impressed.

Charlie Brown's classmates are quite vocal with their opinions: His tree is a flop. While he can't argue that the little sapling needs some yuletide attention, Charlie Brown isn't about to condemn it to the trash heap. But even as he hangs one lone ball on its branches, the poor tree just bends under the weight.

What is he to do?

The kids want only to immerse themselves in the extravagance of the season. Charlie Brown wants only to give a tree some love. And that's when Linus steps in.

Walking up to the microphone in the midst of all the arguing, Linus reads from the Bible the story of the very first Christmas. He tells of the mother and the Baby and the shepherds and the star. He recounts the amazing choir of angels singing glory to God in the highest. And as his words fill the auditorium, a change takes place. The children stop in their tracks. Calm replaces confusion. And that's all that happens. They all gather around Charlie Brown's needy tree and shower it with love. When they step back, the little tree is the most festive, most beautiful, most glowing Christmas tree any of them had ever seen ... just because of its exposure to love. Genuine love truly transforms the ordinary, and that's exactly what we find in today's reading.

The apostles Peter and John had been arrested because of the things they were preaching. Some of the leading priests and Sadducees were upset that they were preaching with authority that there is a resurrection of the dead – a fact that the Sadducees very adamantly denied. Here is how Luke describes it:

> *"The members of the council were amazed when they saw the boldness of Peter and John, for they could see that they were ordinary men who had no special training"* (Acts 4:13a).

These were former fishermen, not theologians or scholars. Yet, we're told that when they were filled with God's Holy Spirit, it made all the difference. Finishing verse 13, let's look at my favourite part.

> *" ... They also recognized them as men who had been with Jesus"* (Acts 4:13b).

These men, in themselves, were nothing special. Like Charlie Brown's tree, they were plain and un-spectacular. But as they were filled with God's Spirit and exposed to His love, they were recognized as men who had been in the presence of Jesus.

What a wonderful way to be known! What a great goal for us! An ordinary person is made extraordinary – simply by soaking in the presence of Jesus.

Come Clean

READ ACTS 4:23-37

Bret Harte tells a story called "The Luck of Roaring Camp." According to the story, Roaring Camp was the meanest, toughest mining town in the West. Murders and thievery were common in this terrible place, inhabited almost entirely by men. Once a young pregnant woman was passing through the town. She didn't intend to stay long, but while there, she died giving birth to a baby girl.

The men of the town were captivated by the baby. They put her into a box, and laid her on top of some old rags. But they decided that didn't look right, so they sent one of the men 80 miles to buy a rosewood cradle. He brought back the cradle, filled it with rags and laid the baby on top. But, that still wasn't right. It didn't seem appropriate for the rags to be there. This time they sent someone to Sacramento, to bring back a beautiful silk and lace blanket.

They then put the baby, wrapped in the blanket, into the rosewood cradle. It looked fine until someone noticed the floor was filthy. So, these tough and hardened men got down on their hands and knees and scrubbed the floor until it was clean. But now the sorry state of the walls, ceiling, and dirty windows without curtains was magnified. So they washed the walls and ceiling and put up curtains. The place looked great. Of course, they had to give up fighting because the baby slept a lot and babies can't sleep during a brawl.

According to Harte the whole atmosphere of Roaring Camp mellowed. Everyone cared for the baby. The men took her cradle to the mine and set it by the entrance so that they all could see her. Then somebody noticed what a barren place it was, so at the mouth of the mine, they planted flowers, making a very nice garden. It looked quite beautiful. As the men daily visited the pristine garden of the baby they became aware of their own filthiness. Soon the general store was sold out of soap, shaving gear and cologne. The baby changed everything.

And so it is with us. Jesus, that Baby born on the first Christmas day, has a way of changing everything. If we let Him, He enters our lives, slips into every crevice, and brings not only righteousness, but *a desire for righteousness*. That is the purpose of the very first Christmas. Just as the believers in the book of Acts prayed,

> "*... everything occurred according to Your eternal will and plan*" (Acts 4:28).

The divine plan of Christmas is to help creation see its filth and then provide a way to come clean. Let the Baby of Christmas in. Accept Jesus as your Saviour, and then marvel at the changes He will bring not only to your *life*, but to your *daily living*.

> *The divine plan of Christmas ... to help creation see its filth ... and then provide a way to come clean.*

Never Box Up Jesus

READ ACTS 5:1-16

In many cultures, the day after Christmas is known as "boxing day." That day is unofficially set aside to box up Christmas trimmings, Christmas trees, children's stockings, and front door wreaths.

When you think about it, it's kind of sad, a letdown, when you finally do have to put all the merriment away. However, according to an article in *Daily Guideposts*, the rest of the year doesn't have to be down at all.

Isabel's husband had been making trips to the attic once again to store the Christmas decorations. The last thing to be put away was the nativity scene from the mantel. She just about had it all packed up. Everything that is, except the manger. "Haven't you finished with that yet?" her husband asked. Isabel, holding the small porcelain baby in her hand said, "I think we'll just leave it out this year. Sometimes the world seems out of control and Christmas seems very far away. When it does, we can look at the mantel and remember that God is with us ..."

Jesus, that Baby in the manger, is Emmanuel, which literally means, *God with us.* Just because we box up our Christmas decorations, it doesn't mean God's Holy Spirit is going anywhere. And that's exactly what we find in today's reading.

The group of believers in Jerusalem was growing and the organization of the Church was developing by leaps and bounds. Meanwhile, the apostles were performing many miraculous wonders among the people. Jesus was no longer with them – the season of Christmas had past. But He left them with His Spirit *and* with the authority that came with a Spirit-controlled life. Luke gives us a taste of what this time was like:

> *"Crowds came in from the villages around Jerusalem, bringing their sick and those possessed by evil spirits, and they were all healed"* (Acts 5:16).

This verse doesn't say that *some* were healed. It says *all* were healed. The powerful Holy Spirit Himself was present and moving through the crowd of hurting people. Most important, He still moves today. Author and speaker Stuart Briscoe had this to say about God's Spirit and the season:

"The spirit of Christmas needs to be superseded by the Spirit of Christ. The spirit of Christmas is annual; the Spirit of Christ is eternal. The spirit of Christmas is sentimental; the Spirit of Christ is supernatural. The spirit of Christmas is a human product; the Spirit of Christ is a divine Person."

Jesus Christ is *God with us,* and He will never be boxed up. We can live with the Spirit of Christ all year long.

"The spirit of Christmas needs to be superseded by the Spirit of Christ. The spirit of Christmas is annual; the Spirit of Christ is eternal. The spirit of Christmas is sentimental; the Spirit of Christ is supernatural. The spirit of Christmas is a human product; the Spirit of Christ is a divine Person."
~ Stuart Briscoe

God's Gift of the Cross

READ ACTS 5:17-33

People can be creative in big ways. From proposing marriage on the Jumbotron at a football stadium, to painting the flag of their country's origin on their home's garage door.

In Wauconda, Illinois two water towers had always served as landmarks, and some 40 years ago the village police chief came up with a holiday idea. He suggested mounting large twin crosses on the towers to radiantly mark the season of Christmas. The idea caught on, and soon the display of crosses became a local tradition. The little community in Illinois took pride in their crosses which silently served as a reminder of the immeasurable love of God shed abroad at Christmas.

However, in 1989 a spokesman for American Atheists, Inc., a man who had never even been to Wauconda, Illinois, heard about the crosses and threatened a law suit. He said that because they were on government property an alleged violation of the separation of Church and state was being committed. He delivered an ultimatum – remove the crosses from the towers, or meet him in court.

The little village called several town meetings. It was noted that Christians and non-Christians in the community were united. They were appalled that some outsider would try and tell them how to celebrate Christmas. But sadly, the decision of what to do was forced by economics. This little town simply could not afford the hundreds of thousands of dollars it would incur in court costs. And so the decision was made, and the two crosses came down.

However, the story didn't end there. The very next morning, after their apparent defeat, the little town showed just who would have the final say. One by one crosses started popping up. Businesses up and down main street all began displaying crosses, and within days they were appearing everywhere – on houses, attached to antennas, stuck in yards, beaming from trees, shining in windows. The media had portrayed this little town as having lost the fight – but they hadn't lost. Two crosses had been replaced with hundreds, and God was glorified in the process.

Opposition to the message of the Cross is something believers in Jesus have always experienced. An as we'll see in todays reading Peter and the apostles found themselves in the middle of some of the very first recorded incidents.

The apostles had been performing many miraculous wonders among the people. Believers began meeting together regularly and people from all over brought to them those who truly needed healing both physically and spiritually – and they were healed. However, the high priest and his friends reacted with violent jealousy. They had the apostles arrested and fiercely ordered them never to teach in the name of Jesus again. Here is Peter's reply:

> *"The God of our ancestors raised up Jesus, the One you killed by hanging Him on a Cross. God set Him on high at His side, Prince and Saviour, to give Israel the gift of a changed life and sins forgiven"* (Acts 5:30-31 *The Message*).

Even under the threat of death, Peter spoke the message of the Cross. There will always be those who turn down their free gift of a new life, just as there will always be those who encourage others to do the same.

Don't let anyone dictate how you respond to the Cross. It is God's gift to you. He wants you to accept it. Embrace the life it gives and then proudly display it.

Embracing the Grind

READ ACTS 5:34 - 42

Recently our daughter's high school broke from business as usual and participated in something called, "Break the Grind Day." Leading up to the stressful days of exams, "Break the Grind Day" gave the kids in the school a rest and a break from the normal routine of structured classes and quiet learning. On this day there was no structure. Kids could basically choose for themselves how to spend their time. From Nintendo playoffs in one room, to Ping Pong tournaments in another, to the movie "Shrek" playing down the hall – this was a day out of the ordinary. In fact, when Andrea left for school that morning, she didn't even look like a student. It wasn't until I waved good-bye to her from the front door that I noticed she was wearing her plaid flannel jammies and leopard-print fuzzy slippers. If Andrea was going to break from routine, she wasn't going to do it half-heartedly. And that's the way many of her friends showed up at school (thankfully!).

All 1500 students in the high school were encouraged to forget life as usual and "break the grind" for a day. Kind of like removing your foot from the accelerator for awhile and coasting. But what happens when someone adopts this position as a way of life? When a Christian, for instance, chooses to *reject* the grind and coast in their faith, never preparing for "exams" that are sure to come? Thankfully, that was an option Peter and the apostles never entertained.

In Acts chapter 5, we find that Peter and some of the apostles had been arrested – again – for preaching in Jesus' name. Even in shackles before the high council, Peter proclaimed the truth of the Cross and the gift of God's grace. This made council members so furious that they decided to kill the apostles. Only by intervention of a Pharisee named Gamaliel were they not executed that day.

He was convinced that if the apostles were freed, their little following would disburse. But also he knew that if they were of God, no force on earth could suppress their voice. And we know, his prediction proved true – they were of God, and their voices live on. Peter and the apostles were freed that day and we read:

> *"The apostles left the high council rejoicing that God had counted them worthy to suffer dishonour for the name of Jesus"* (Acts 5:41).

I can't help but marvel at their attitude. The apostles weren't even upset at their imprisonment. Instead they were honoured to suffer for Jesus! Which of us would see suffering as an honour? Would we see "the grind" of our faith – those hardships we *will* face through our association with Jesus – as something to be *accepted* instead of *avoided*? Billy Graham had an opinion on this:

> *"Within the New Testament, there is no indication that Christians should expect to be healthy, wealthy, and successful in this present age. Christ told His disciples to expect to have troubles. This age is interested in success, not suffering. We can identify with James and John who wanted choice seats in the kingdom. We might even ask for reclining chairs and soft music."*

The apostles counted themselves honoured to be found worthy to suffer for Jesus. They rejoiced at the prospect of persecution. That kind of attitude does not "break" the grind. It embraces it.

The Extraordinary Power of God

READ ACTS 6:1-15

The last day of the year. It's a time to look back and re-live the year's best moments, and a time to reflect back upon the year's worst. Some years seem to take more than their fair share of devastating moments – and the pain they've left seems to command our attention. But we know that no matter how far we travel from the pain of the past, "staring" into its glare will always hurt our eyes. That's why a story told by a certain pastor seemed so fitting.

David Peterson, a Presbyterian pastor in Spokane, Washington, told about a time when he was in his office preparing a sermon. His little daughter came in and said, "Daddy, can we play?"

He said to her, "I'm awfully sorry, sweetheart, but I'm right in the middle of preparing this sermon. In about an hour I can play." She smiled at him and said, "Okay, Daddy, but when you're finished I'm going to give you a great big hug."

He said she went to the door and to quote him, "did a U-turn and came back and gave me a chiropractic, bone-breaking hug." Her father said to her, "Darling, you said you were going to give me a hug *after* I finish." With a twinkle in her eye, his little girl answered, "Daddy, I just wanted you to know what you have to look forward to!"

Looking forward. Sometimes we just need to be reminded of where our focus should be. The apostle Stephen gave us a glowing example of what it means for us as followers of Jesus to be able to look forward in difficult circumstances.

The early Christian Church was growing so fast that some organizational guidelines had to be established. The apostles needed to spend their time in prayer and preaching and teaching about Jesus. Because of this, out of the thousands of believers seven men were selected to be deacons. Their job was to look after the everyday work of the Church. These men had to be well respected and full of the Holy Spirit and of wisdom. Stephen was one of those men. Not only was he busy with his duties as a deacon, but verse eight tells us that he was also performing "amazing miracles and signs among the people."

Stephen's ministry caused quite a stir among those who belonged to the Jewish synagogue. These learned men entered into debate with Stephen, an ordinary man who was "full of God's grace and power." Here is what happened:

> *"But they were not able to resist the intelligence and the wisdom and [the inspiration of] the Spirit with which and by Whom he spoke"* (Acts 6:10 *The Amplified Bible*).

Stephen, an ordinary man, was filled with God's extraordinary Spirit and had the ability to speak under the Holy Spirit's anointing:

> *"Then all who sat in the council (Sanhedrin), as they gazed intently at Stephen, saw that his face had the appearance of the face of an angel"* (Acts 6:15 *The Amplified Bible*).

Stephen was a common man who moved in the uncommon supernatural power of God simply because of his obedience. And it's available for us too. As we move forward in obedience and allow God's power to flow through us, just think of all that we have to look forward to!

Beyond the Comfort Zone

READ ACTS 7:1-22

How do you "expand your horizons"? Live a healthier lifestyle? Readjust your focus? Enlarge your comfort zone?

According to the "physically fit" among us, all of these things can be accomplished if we'll just get outdoors more. Go on walks. Take hikes. Commune with nature. That seems to be the trend. Yet the notes in the suggestion box at the famous Bridger Wilderness Area paint a different picture.

Spanning almost a half million acres, this majestic landscape boasts virtually untouched terrain along the Continental Divide in the state of Wyoming. It's a governmentally regulated area "affected primarily by the forces of nature, where man is a visitor who does not remain." But according to some comment cards visitors have given staff members, you would think they expected to find the comforts of home:

- Trails need to be wider so people can walk while holding hands.
- Trails need to be reconstructed. Please avoid building trails that go uphill.
- Too many bugs and spiders and spider webs. Please spray the wilderness to rid of these pests.
- The coyotes made too much noise last night and kept me awake. Please eradicate these annoying animals.
- The places where trails *do not* exist aren't well marked.
- And finally, There are too many rocks in the mountains.

Instead of *stretching* their endurance, these people wanted to compact the vast wilderness into their comfort zones. Oh, the growth they miss by doing this!

Moving outside our comfort zones isn't easy for most of us. But in the end it brings eternal benefits.

In today's reading we see that the apostle Stephen had been arrested and was standing on trial before the Jewish High Priest. As we discovered in chapter six, Stephen was a godly man, full of faith and God's Holy Spirit. Was it easy for Stephen to let go of the control of his will and allow a Higher Power to have His say? I don't know. But I do know that as Stephen answered the false accusations of blasphemy against him, he was not on his own. We can be confident that the words Stephen spoke were given by the Spirit of God. So, what did he say?

Stephen began his address by recounting the life of someone these Jewish leaders would have known well. He recounted to them the words of God to Abraham, a very ordinary, yet pivotal man in Jewish history. Words that demanded much faith from Abraham:

> *"God told him, 'Leave your native land and your relatives, and come to the land that I will show you'"* (Acts 7:3).

God encouraged Abraham to step away from the familiar and to trust Him. And this walk of faith became a legacy to us. Similarly, Stephen left us a legacy of faith when he was on trial for a crime punishable by death. When he was given an opportunity to defend himself, he expounded on the faithfulness of God. In taking the stand at his trial, Stephen took a stand for his Lord. In so doing, he entered his own uncertain and potentially frightening "wilderness." But by faith Stephen was sure it would lead him home.

What does moving outside of our comfort zones require? For starters we have to "take a hike" outside of the comfort of the familiar into the *real comfort* of a relationship with God. And when we do that, we'll find that our comfort zone has truly grown as big as all outdoors.

The Satisfier of the Soul

READ ACTS 7:23-36

As he stood before a hostile religious tribunal, the apostle Stephen continued his sermon on God's faithfulness. He began his address by recounting the life of Abraham, the father of Isaac who was in turn the father of Jacob, the father of the Jewish nation. Stephen then expounded on the life of Moses, calling him "a beautiful child in God's eyes." Concerning the Hebrew baby raised by the Egyptian Pharaoh's daughter, Stephen said:

> *"Moses was taught all the wisdom of the Egyptians, and he became mighty in both speech and action"* (Acts 7:22).

By outward indications, Moses had a promising future. He was highly educated and probably well respected. No one could have predicted the desert experience that awaited this rising star. In defending a fellow Hebrew, he killed a man and escaped into the desert to avoid punishment. For 40 long years, Moses lived in empty discouragement. He married and raised a family in the dust-bowl existence of a spiritually parched man too scared to search for refreshing water. Until one day, the "Water" came to him.

In the desert near Mount Sinai Moses came face to face with the Satisfier of his soul, surprisingly, in the form of a burning bush. This is what happened when Moses encountered the miraculous bush:

> *"As he went to see, the voice of the Lord called out to him, 'I am the God of your ancestors — the God of Abraham, Isaac, and Jacob.' Moses shook with terror and dared not look. And the Lord said to him, 'Take off your sandals, for you are standing on holy ground'"* (Acts 7:31-33).

This highly educated man required a supernatural event from God to get his attention, and that's not all. God also had to spell out for Moses his proper reaction to God's Presence – one of humble respect. As Moses finally drank from the well of God's holiness, he was transformed from a shepherd on the back-side of a desert to a man of God's destiny. No longer satisfied to tend sheep for his father-in-law, Moses now desired to shepherd the "lost sheep" of Israel for his Father in Heaven. All because of a dramatic encounter with God.

We too may feel like our life may have gone off course, or as Bugs Bunny says, "taken a wrong turn in Albuquerque" – and wound up in the Sahara. As author Robert Short observed, we have:

> *"Lots of knowledge, but little understanding*
> *Lots of means, but little meaning*
> *Lots of know-how, but little know-why, and*
> *Lots of sight, but little insight."*

And hence, our desert-wanderings. In our information-overloaded world, how are we to sift through it all and find true meaning? In the early part of the last century, renowned theologian A.W. Tozer commented on our dilemma:

> *"Modern mankind can go anywhere, do everything and be completely curious about the universe. But only a rare person is curious enough to want to know God."*

To want to know God. To search our desert until we find the original "Spring of Life" – the only Satisfier of the soul. His name is Jesus. He told the woman at the well the truth, "The water I give takes away thirst altogether ... it becomes a perpetual spring within ... giving eternal life" (*John 4:14*).

Is your inner life a dust-bowl? Is your soul dry and barren? You will never be satisfied until you come to the One who can quench your thirst. Not just today, but forever.

Our Hidden Treasure

READ ACTS 7:37-60

The May 17, 1987 issue of *The Atlanta Journal Constitution*, featured a story about Rob Cutshaw, a North Carolina "rock hound." He owned a little roadside shop where he sold rocks from nearby caves and hills. He readily admitted to being no rock expert, only claiming to know enough about rocks to recognize what was nice enough to sell to collectors and jewelry makers. As much as he enjoyed his work, Rob admitted it didn't always pay the bills.

But while on a dig some 20 years ago, Rob found a rock that even he could tell was valuable. He tried unsuccessfully to sell the specimen, and according to the newspaper article, kept the rock under his bed. Rob thought the blue chunk could bring as much as $500, but he would have taken less if something urgent came up, like paying his electric bill. For 20 years, Rob Cutshaw went to bed every night with the stone beneath him, but only when he was face to face with an expert did he discover that his blue rock was nearly priceless. After the large stone was cut and polished and named "The Star of David Sapphire," it weighed nearly a pound and could easily sell for just under three million dollars.

And so it is with us. Often we do not realize the full glory of the treasure we possess as followers of Jesus. If hidden away, the value of eternal hope He gives can be diminished when buried beneath life's diversions.

Not so with Stephen. For when he was brought face to face with a tribunal of Jewish leaders, he spoke boldly of the faithfulness of God. At the end of his address he shifted from proclaiming God's goodness to exposing man's evil. In doing so, he revealed the central message of Christianity – the truth that all have sinned and are lost apart from the sacrifice of Jesus.

Stephen's message enraged the Jewish leaders who, in their fury, expressed their lust for blood. You would think Stephen would have been terrified looking into eyes filled with such violent hatred. Instead, his attention was drawn to something of far greater eternal significance:

> *"But Stephen, full of the Holy Spirit, looked up to heaven and saw the glory of God, and Jesus standing at the right hand of God. 'Look,' he said, 'I see heaven open and the Son of Man standing at the right hand of God!'"* (Acts 7:55, 56).

Stephen, in mortal danger because of what he believed, saw a glimpse of the Treasure in Whom he believed. In that instant, he came face-to-face with his precious Saviour and the knowledge that whatever happened next was in God's full control. And what did happen next? These incensed men, filled with violent hatred, dragged Stephen out of the city and stoned him – but not before Stephen realized the amazing value of his trust in God. Stephen exemplified a faithful life fully realizing its reward.

One more thing. If you look closely at the end of verse 58, you'll notice someone guarding the coats of Stephen's murderers. He was a young man named Saul, later known as the beloved apostle Paul. And this gives us a glimpse of just how far God's grace can bring a man, and just how mighty he can become.

Author Calvin Miller once said that "the world is poor because her treasure is buried in the sky and all her treasure maps are of the earth." For the most part, he's right ... all the maps but One. God's Word is our map to the most valuable treasure of all – the pathway back to God. And that pathway is only through the Cross of His Son.

Safe in God's Love

READ ACTS 8:1-13

The life of a believer in Christ in 1930's Russia was difficult. In the bustling town of Stavropol, Communist leader Stalin had ordered that all Bibles be confiscated and its Christian citizens sent to prison camps. Ironically, most of the Bibles were not destroyed, yet many Christians died as "enemies of the state." Author Ken Taylor tells this story about those enduring Bibles.

In 1994, well after the dissolution of the Soviet Union, a Christian missions team arrived in the now-liberated town of Stavropol. They had arranged for Bibles to be shipped to Moscow and then to Stavropol for distribution, but their shipment had been caught at customs in red tape. Someone then told them about a warehouse outside of town where confiscated Bibles were still stored. Remarkably, the team was given permission to take them and distribute them. After hiring several local Russian workers, the team began loading the trucks with the dusty Bibles.

One local young man, a cynical and bitter individual, agreed to work, but he let it be known that his motivation was only for the days' wages. As the day progressed, some of the workers noticed that the angry young man had disappeared. It wasn't until much later that he was discovered in the corner of the warehouse weeping like a baby, an open Bible in his hands. Intending to steal it and later sell it, the young man had picked a worn and tattered Bible that turned out to have been his own grandmother's. Her signature was aged, but clearly visible on the front page. And as he had read the life-changing words of that Book, his heart had begun to change. He was remarkably transformed by the very Bible for which his grandmother had been persecuted – the very Bible on which he would now base his life.

That's the transforming power of God's Holy Spirit. Once He's touched a life, no tribulation on earth can stop His mighty flow. And this is a fact that the believers in our reading for today knew all too well.

The apostle Stephen, an ordinary man full of God's transforming Spirit, had just been murdered for his beliefs, making him the first martyr for the Christian Church. This day also marked for the followers of Jesus the beginning of the devastating trials that Jesus spoke of in John 15.

> *"A great wave of persecution began that day, sweeping over the church in Jerusalem, and all the believers except the apostles fled into Judea and Samaria ... the believers who had fled Jerusalem went everywhere preaching the Good News about Jesus"* (Acts 8:1,4).

"A great wave of persecution" – that's what these people endured because of their stand for Jesus. And yet even while running from certain death, they preached the Good News of eternal life. Why did they do this? How could the early followers of Jesus have such courage and live so boldly in the face of danger? Simple. Their devotion wasn't to a cause, but to a Person – Jesus, God in flesh. They knew that ultimately His invincible love would never let them down. Listen to the way the apostle Paul said it:

> *"I am convinced that nothing can ever separate us from [God's] love. Death can't, and life can't ... our fears for today, our worries about tomorrow, and even the powers of hell can't keep God's love away"* (Romans 8:38).

Paul powerfully conveys that when you readily embrace suffering for Jesus, you never leave the safety of His arms. The persecuted Church of the 1930's knew this, just as we do today. To go through life knowing without a doubt, that whatever may come our way we are totally and completely safe in God's love.

Just a Little Can't Hurt?

READ ACTS 8:14-25

The concept of sin can be a difficult thing to grasp. We know its contamination is all around us, so how do we keep it from getting into us? Is it even possible to stay free from sin? One creative father very vividly illustrated for his children the importance of doing just that.

It seems his teenage children had taken on a kind of laid-back view of sin. Their motto for the most part was, just a little sin can't hurt! His motto was, sin is sin and should be avoided, period! They thought he was hyper-sensitive, and he knew they weren't sensitive enough. This was an ongoing debate that their father just couldn't win. That is, until he stopped trying to win with words.

One afternoon, when his teens got home from school "starving" for a snack, their father was waiting for them with a fresh-from-the-oven batch of brownies. They looked delicious. As the kids took one, their fingers sank into the soft warmth of the chocolate treat. Mmmmm! They were about to take their first bite when their dad spoke up.

"Before you take a bite, I must tell you I altered the recipe slightly." The brownies stopped in mid-air. "Just before I poured the batter into the pan," their father said, "I went into the backyard and collected a little bit of doggie doo-doo, and I baked it into the brownies. It wasn't much. I can't remember the exact amount. No matter. As you say about sin, 'just a little can't hurt!' So, eat up!" Needless to say, not one of them took a bite. Whether in large doses or small, sin is sin and will always have a devastating effect. That was the same message from the apostle Peter.

Peter and John had been travelling the countryside spreading the Good News of the message of Jesus. Whenever they preached, people not only came to believe in Jesus, they also received the gift of His Holy Spirit that filled them to overflowing with God's power. But not everyone the apostles met understood the message of the selfless love of Jesus or the free gift of God's Spirit. Such was a man known as Simon:

> *"A man named Simon had been a sorcerer there for many years, claiming to be someone great. The Samaritan people, from the least to the greatest, often spoke of him as "the Great One ..."* (Acts 8:9, 10).

Simon had a large following, and a large ego as well. Although he became a follower of the apostle Philip, we learn that his transformation didn't go very deep. When Peter and John arrived operating in the power of God's Spirit, instead of "standing" in awe, Simon made them a "standing offer." Promising them money, he said, "Let me have this power too."

Simon wanted to buy a gift from God to make himself great. Not a huge sin as some sin is measured, but enough to reveal a contaminated heart. From his response we see that Peter saw this clearly:

> *"Turn from your wickedness and pray to the Lord. Perhaps He will forgive your evil thoughts, for I can see that you are full of bitterness and held captive by sin"* (Acts 8:22, 23).

Just how much sin can hold a person captive? As with the brownies, contamination doesn't take much. However, unlike the brownies we do not have to remain contaminated forever. Through the Cross of Jesus we have forgiveness. Through the Gift of His Spirit, we have power. And through our Heavenly Father, we have love – amazing love that cleanses us from contamination and transforms us by His grace. Now that's something you can sink your teeth into!

The Most Important Story

READ ACTS 8:26-40

Charles Berry was a renowned English preacher in the 19th century. Although he became known as a mighty man of God, Berry's ministry started in weakness. He admittedly preached a very thin Gospel. Berry looked upon Jesus as merely a noble teacher *of* life, not a divine Redeemer *to* life. Gordon MacDonald told this story of the night Pastor Berry came face-to-face with one soul's desperate need for a Saviour.

Late one evening during his first pastorate a young girl came to his door. "Are you a minister?" she asked. When he nodded yes, she hurriedly said, "You must come with me quickly. I want you to get my Mother in."

Thinking it was a case of a drunken woman in the streets, Berry said, "You must go and get a policeman."

"No," said the girl, "my Mother is dying, and you must come and get her into heaven."

And so, the minister followed the girl through the dark and lonely streets. Finally reaching her mother, Berry knelt beside her and told the dying woman how good and kind Jesus had been and how He'd come to show us how to live. She cut him off sharply. "Mister," she cried, "that's no use for the likes of me. I'm a sinner. Can't you tell me of someone who can have mercy upon me and save my poor soul?"

Later sharing this story, Berry said, "I stood there in the presence of a dying woman and I realized I had nothing to tell her. In the midst of sin and death, I had no message." Then he told how he had remembered a story he had learned at his Mother's knee of the Cross and of a Christ who is able to save anybody. Tears ran down the woman's cheeks. "Now you're getting it," she said. "Now you're helping me." Berry himself later said, "I got her in, and blessed be God, I got in myself."

The purity of the undiluted message of mercy that is the Cross. People not only *need* to hear it, they *want* to hear it. And just as an English pastor found that to be true, so did a first century evangelist.

Philip the evangelist was one of Jesus' many followers who fled for his life from the city of Jerusalem and "went everywhere preaching the Good News about Jesus." After ministering in the city of Samaria, Philip was instructed by an angel where to go next, and went immediately. That's when he came upon the treasurer of Ethiopia, a eunuch of great authority under the queen of Ethiopia. Seeing him seated in the back of his carriage,

> *"Philip ran over and heard the man reading from the prophet Isaiah; so he asked, 'Do you understand what you are reading?' The man replied, 'How can I, when there is no one to instruct me?' And he begged Philip to come up into the carriage and sit with him"* (Acts 8:29-31).

What was the Scripture this man was reading? It was Isaiah 53:7-8:

> *"He was led as a sheep to the slaughter. And as a lamb is silent before the shearers, he did not open his mouth"* (Isaiah 53:7).

It was the story of Jesus. Just as did the dying woman with Charles Berry, this man begged Philip to tell him about the Saviour of his soul. The straightforward, undiluted message of the Cross – it's the message that millions are dying to hear. It's the most important story we can ever tell.

A Wonderful Life

READ ACTS 9:1-19

Have you ever noticed how people will react in many different ways to the very same experience?

Recently, our family watched one of my all-time favourite movies, the Christmas classic, "It's a Wonderful Life." You know the story. George Baily, played by Jimmy Stewart, had a wonderful life, that is, until his uncle misplaced $8,000, making George accountable. George deemed his life to be over. But Clarence, his guardian angel, stepped in to remind George that all was not lost.

The ending is the best part of the movie. George ran into the house to find his wife. He hugged and kissed his kids and shook hands with the man who came to arrest him. George was a changed man. And when his wife arrived home, she didn't come alone. George's friends had heard that he was in trouble and the whole town came to help. While singing, "Hark the Herald Angels Sing," George's friends showered him with love *and* with money. And the look of gratitude in George's eyes was profound.

As the closing scene faded, we all reacted differently. Our 15-year-old daughter smiled and said it was great. Our 12-year-old son thought it was "kinda long" while our youngest son just grunted in his sleep. Ron chuckled as the singers belted out their song, and I sat in the corner of the couch crying like a baby.

Of course, I've seen it before. And yes, I knew exactly how it would end. And yes, I always cry at the same spot – my family never fails to remind me of that. Each of us reacted differently to the very same experience. And exposure to God's presence is no different.

Today's passage is pivotal in the life of the early Church, but more precisely, pivotal in the life of a man named Saul. Saul was the "young witness" to the murder of Stephen. He was a "well-connected man" eager to destroy everyone linked to Jesus. Saul was a bitter man on an evil mission – one that eventually brought him face-to-face with his destiny. We read:

> *"As he was nearing Damascus on this mission, a brilliant light from heaven suddenly beamed down upon him! He fell to the ground and heard a voice saying to him, 'Saul! Saul! Why are you persecuting me?' 'Who are you, sir?' Saul asked. And the voice replied, 'I am Jesus, the One you are persecuting!"* (Acts 9:3-5).

On the Damascus road Saul came face-to-face with Jesus. When confronted with God's Presence people always react, but not all react the same way. For example, at the burning bush Moses "hid his face in his hands because he was afraid to look at God" (*Exodus 3:6*). Or as his life was ending, the apostle Stephen "gazed steadily upward" (*Acts 7:55*).

And then there was Saul. Reading in the first part of verse six and then verse eight, let's hear his reaction to God's Presence.

> *"So he, trembling and astonished, said, "Lord, what do You want me to do? ... As Saul picked himself up off the ground, he found that he was blind."* (Acts 9:6a NKJV and 8 NLT).

Saul was a tough case. While we're not told why God blinded him, we know the end result. The trembling and astonished man who lost his sight on the road was not the same man who found it again three days later. We see the transformation in Saul when Ananias obeyed God's voice and went to pray for Saul. As he did, God not only touched Saul physically, He transformed him spiritually as He filled Saul with His Holy Spirit.

Although each of us reacts differently when exposed to God's Presence, perhaps the most important thing of all is that we *are* in His Presence. As we go there regularly, He truly does give us "a wonderful life."

He is Always Bigger

READ ACTS 9:20-31

When the world focused on *The Lord of the Rings* trilogy and its author, J. R. R. Tolkien, there seemed to be a renewed interest in a contemporary of his, renowned author, C. S. Lewis. As you may know, C. S. Lewis wrote many well-known books such as *The Problem With Pain*, *Mere Christianity* and *The Screwtape Letters*. He often wrote in the same metaphorical style as Tolkien, however Lewis was more straight forward with his symbolism. His characters and their counterparts are more easily recognizable. One such character is the lion Aslan from his popular *Chronicles of Narnia*, series. Aslan, as the ruler of Narnia, is majestic, wise, strong, and a terrifying mystery to those who do not know him. He is a powerful image of the real Lion of Judah – a name given to Christ. In *Prince Caspian* the second book of the *Narnia* series, Lewis powerfully alludes to our view of God.

In the story, Lucy, one of the human children who originally discovered the land of Narnia, is older now and has once again returned to this enchanted place. She hasn't seen Aslan in quite a while, and their reunion is sweet. Lucy says to the lion who represents Christ, "Aslan, you're bigger now." An unusual occurrence, because for the most part when we revisit places from our childhood their once considerable status shrinks with the sharp focus of our older, more mature eyes. But that's not the case here, as Aslan points out. "Lucy," Aslan, the Christ figure, says, "that's because you are older. You see, every year that you grow, you will find me bigger."

And so it is with us. As you and I grow and mature in our relationship with God, we will find Him bigger in His faithfulness, bigger in His holiness and bigger in His grace. And that will make our growth all the sweeter, as Saul of Tarsus learned.

A renowned enemy of the Church, Saul had just had an incredible experience – a direct encounter with the Saviour, Jesus, that left him blind for three days. Because of the obedience of a believer named Ananias to pray for him, Saul was not only touched physically, but transformed spiritually by a complete invasion of God's Holy Spirit. How did Saul react?

> *"And immediately he began preaching about Jesus in the synagogues, saying, 'He is indeed the Son of God!'"* (Acts 9:20).

After his 'rebirth' through God's Spirit, Saul eagerly began his journey to spiritual maturity. Not everyone trusted him at first. His reputation of cruelty was widely known among the Christians. But because of the witness of a man named Barnabas, Saul was accepted among the growing body of believers. And with his inclusion came a reprieve in their suffering.

> *"The church then had peace throughout Judea, Galilee, and Samaria, and it grew in strength and numbers. The believers were walking in the fear of the Lord and in the comfort of the Holy Spirit"* (Acts 9:31).

As the Church's vision of God increased, it grew in peace, in strength, and in number. So what does that mean to us? Life isn't always peaceful, and we're not always strong. Sometimes it seems that no amount of growth can stand up to devastating circumstances that come our way. When they do, how do we react? All we can do is look to almighty God and in faith know that no matter what threatens our peace – He is always bigger.

The Source of Life

READ ACTS 9:32-43

Certain dates on the calendar will always have a story to tell. They're an interruption on mankind's time line that reminds us that our focus should be on God, our Source of life. Important dates such as July 1st – the day that Canada spread her wings. Or December 7th – a "date that will live in infamy." And of course no one will ever forget September 11th – the day our very freedom was attacked. So what about April 30th? That date may ring a bell, but only for the most astute in American history. With the following words, President Abraham Lincoln designated April 30th 1863, as a day of national humiliation, fasting, and prayer:

> *"It is the duty of nations, as well as of men, who owe their dependence upon the overruling power of God, to confess their sins and transgressions in humble sorrow and to recognize the sublime truth that those nations only are blessed whose God is the Lord."*

President Lincoln made this proclamation while his country was in the middle of its greatest time of sorrow – the American Civil War. Read on with me words of wisdom that can only come from experience, and allow the years to melt away as you hear his timeless warning:

> *"Intoxicated with unbroken success, we have become too self-sufficient to feel the necessity of redeeming and preserving grace, too proud to pray to the God that made us. We have grown in numbers, wealth, and power as no other nation has grown, but we have forgotten God."*

A lesson from one country's past to another country's future. Don't forget God. Go back to the only Source of Life. It sometimes takes life's most devastating moments to drive us to where we should have been all along – on our knees. Such is the case now, and such was the case in the day of the apostles.

The apostle Peter was a mighty man of God who lived and travelled with Jesus before the Cross and preached life-giving forgiveness through Jesus afterward. Peter received the gift of God's Holy Spirit on the day of Pentecost and then boldly travelled the country bringing help and healing where it was needed. One place he visited was the city of Joppa. A much-loved believer there named Tabitha had become sick and died, and many people mourned for her. However, when they heard that the renowned apostle Peter was nearby, they sent word begging him to come. They had heard of the power of the apostles and had hoped that Peter could perform a miracle. When he arrived they eagerly took him to where the body lay. But what did the acclaimed "miracle worker" do?

> *"But Peter asked them all to leave the room; then he knelt and prayed"* (Acts 9:40a).

The mighty man of God knew where to go for life. This "interruption" in Peter's timeline drove him to his knees, and then,

> *"Turning to the body he said, 'Get up, Tabitha.' And she opened her eyes! When she saw Peter, she sat up!"* (Acts 9:40b).

The dead woman came to life! And it wasn't because Tabitha was special or because Peter was holy. She came to life because God is God. The great "Source *of* Life" was her "Source *for* Life." We don't understand it, and we sure can't explain it. But I have a feeling that Tabitha, no explanation was needed. All that mattered was that she was alive.

The same is true with us. In our sin we are dead. When we come to God through Jesus we come alive. How? We are literally connecting to the Source of Life. And no matter what day you make that connection, it will be a day worth remembering.

Let's Roll

READ ACTS 10:1-8

The beginning of Acts chapter 10 introduces us to a Roman army officer named Cornelius. God used this man who was a gentile to teach a very vital lesson to the apostle Peter. It is therefore important to know exactly what kind of man Cornelius was. From this passage we learn that:

> *"He was a thoroughly good man. He had led everyone in his house to live worshipfully before God, was always helping people in need, and had the habit of prayer"* (Acts 10:2 *The Message Bible*).

Cornelius was a man of integrity. How many men do you know who are honest, upright, and selflessly committed to both God and family? When you really think about it, not many people fit that description. Someone who did, however, was Todd Beamer, a committed Christian, and one of the passengers on the September 11th United Flight #93.

The week before September 11th Todd and his wife Lisa spent a romantic getaway in Italy. The couple returned home on Monday just in time for Todd to catch his Tuesday morning flight. He was planning on spending more time with his two young sons, ages three and one when he returned. But, as history tells us, that never happened.

About 90 minutes into the westbound flight, the Boeing 757 was hijacked by terrorists, and immediately forced to make a sharp turn south. Todd reached for the GTE airfone in the back of one of the seats and spoke to a supervisor on the ground. He explained what was happening and indicated that he and the other passengers would likely not survive. She then explained to him what had already happened at the World Trade Center and the Pentagon.

Hearing this, Todd must have realized that the hijackers were intending to do something similar with his plane. Even though the hijacker nearest to Todd had a bomb strapped around his waste. Todd, a man of high moral conviction stated that he and a few others would do their best to prevent the terrorists from succeeding. He then asked the person on the phone to call his wife and tell her every word of their conversation, and how much he loved her. Before hanging up, this committed Christian and devoted family man who taught Sunday school every week, asked the person on the phone to pray the Lord's Prayer with him. With the sound of passengers screaming in the background, she complied. When they finished the prayer, Todd calmly said, "Help me, God. Help me, Jesus." Still listening on her end of the phone, the GTE employee then heard Todd say to some of the other passengers, "Are you ready guys? Let's roll!" With that, the phone went dead. What happened next was a testimony to their courage. Within a few minutes, Flight 93 nose-dived into a rural field 80 miles outside of Pittsburgh leaving a crater 40 feet deep.

Men of high moral conviction who know what's right, and do it, are not hard to spot. They cast a shadow of godliness that's impossible to miss. Just as this story is a beautiful memorial to Todd Beamer, so is our verse for today for an officer named Cornelius.

If someone were to look at us for traces of godliness, what would they see? Oswald Chambers once said, "Where there is a vision [of God], there is also a life of honesty and integrity, because the vision gives the moral incentive."

Have a living, intimate vision of God, and then live a life that lets the world know you do.

That They Will Be One

READ ACTS 10:9-33

The Olympics! They happen every two years. That's when the countries of the world gather their finest athletes and compete as equals for the coveted gold medal. Race and nationality aside, attention is drawn solely to the competitors' talents. But that wasn't always the case. In the 1936 Olympic games in Berlin, Germany, there was at least one competitor who was far from Hitler's idea of a sterling athlete. His name was Jesse Owens and he was an African-American. It meant little to Nazi Germany that Owens had set three world records in one day the year before. And Jesse Owens understood this. As he walked to the long jump pit, he saw a tall, blue-eyed blond German taking practice jumps. Owens was well aware how eager the Nazis were to prove their theory of "Aryan superiority." The pressure was overwhelming and on his first jump he overshot the foul line by several inches. Rattled, he did the same on his second attempt. Jesse Owens was only one foul away from being eliminated when the incredible happened.

The tall German walked over to Owens and introduced himself as Luz Long. And that's when the white specimen of Nazi manhood and the black son of a sharecropper chatted in view of the entire stadium. A buzz rippled through the crowd.

What were they talking about? Apparently, since the qualifying distance was a full three feet shorter than what Owens usually jumped, Long suggested he make a mark several inches before the foul line and jump from there just to play it safe.

Amazing! This was the beginning of WWII, and these men were supposedly enemies, yet one was helping the other with words of encouragement.

Owens qualified easily. In the finals he set an Olympic record and earned one of his four gold medals. And the first person to congratulate him was Luz Long – in full view of Adolf Hitler. Owens later wrote, "You could melt down all the medals and cups I have, and they wouldn't be plating on the 24-carat friendship I felt for Luz Long."

In our humanness we all find common ground if we look past the outward. What a good lesson for us – and as we'll see in today's reading, a good lesson for the apostle Peter.

An angel told Cornelius, a gentile of utmost integrity, to send for the Jewish apostle Peter. In the meantime, Peter was also hearing from God. In a vision Peter saw a sheet lowered down from Heaven. In it was every kind of creature. A voice told Peter to "get up, kill and eat." To do this would have been a violation of Jewish religious law – something even a liberated believer in Christ like Peter was reluctant to do. Yet God repeated the vision three times, driving home the message of unconditional acceptance. After that he received an invitation to the home of Cornelius. Reading from verse 28, let's hear the words of Peter as he stepped into a gentile home for the first time in his life.

> *"Peter told them, 'You know it is against the Jewish laws for me to come into a Gentile home like this. But God has shown me that I should never think of anyone as impure'"* (Acts 10:28).

For centuries Jews and Gentiles were not a good mix – but the Cross of Jesus changed that. Listen to part of the prayer of Jesus for all believers the night before He went to the Cross.

> *"My prayer for all of them is that they will be one, just as You and I are one, Father ..."* (John 17:21a).

Shades of colour. Images of race. They all melt away when the Blood of Jesus covers us. In the end that is the only mark of distinction that matters.

The Privilege of Intimacy

READ ACTS 10:34-48

Last summer my Mom, my husband and I spent an entire day going through some boxes in our garage. This may not sound very exciting to you, but it proved to be a gold mine to me. These were boxes of my father's things, and sorting them was a task we had put off for several months after he passed away.

As we soon discovered, Dad was a pack-rat. That discovery meant a lot to me because so am I. Among his many stacks of books and papers, I found some treasures – not in a monetary sense – but treasures just the same from my father's younger days. These special items were reminders of the things he accomplished before I knew him. For instance, in one box I found his high school diploma from 1950, its black leather case still in good condition. The diploma is proof that my Dad passed his courses and graduated from high school.

And then there were his dog tags from the Army. They are imprinted with Dad's name, serial number, and religious affiliation, and they accompanied him on many trips into the back roads of Korea and the jungles of Viet Nam. These two treasures are tributes to my Dad's brave determination. When he presented them to the appropriate people, they earned him privileges and opened doors. Now they are mine.

But if I took his diploma to a university campus and applied for enrollment, would I be accepted? It is a valid high school diploma, but I didn't earn it.

What about the dog tags? Could I bring them into the Veterans Association and expect to get a pension? What I'd probably get would be remarks I couldn't repeat. No, I did nothing to earn these credentials and other than giving me an eternal connection to my father, they are of no earthly good to me. And fortunately for us, when it comes to a connection to our Heavenly Father, salvation doesn't require any earthly credentials.

The apostle Peter, a Jew, was in the home of Cornelius, a gentile – something Peter would readily admit was unheard of. But he was there in obedience to God. In fact, Cornelius had invited many there because he had been told by an angel that Peter would come with a message. The message he spoke was broadly inclusive, extending far beyond the boundaries of race or religion:

> *"I see very clearly that God doesn't show partiality. In every nation He accepts those who fear Him and do what is right ... And no doubt you know that God anointed Jesus of Nazareth with the Holy Spirit and with power ... He is the One all the prophets testified about, saying that everyone who believes in Him will have their sins forgiven through His name"*
> (Acts 10:34, 35, 38a, 43).

God's acceptance of humankind through the Cross is universal. Jesus' death on the Cross was more than a sacrifice that liberates us in this life. It was an act that affects our future. If we allow it to do so, the cleansing Blood of Jesus shed on the Cross will cut through our imperfect past, until all that is left is a forgiven person in the presence of a Holy God. A person with "Blood-bought" credentials. That is the unconditional message of God's grace. We didn't earn the privilege of intimacy with Him, yet He freely gives it because of His love.

If you let it, this privilege of intimacy will not only connect you to the God of your Father, it will ensure that in Him you have a hope-filled future.

Welcome to His Table

READ ACTS 11:1-18

Large families can be a blessing. They may be a little chaotic at times, but definitely a blessing – especially when it comes to a holiday meal.

In the Mainse family – there are 26 members, if you include all the grandchildren – and on special occasions we all eat together. Because we are so many, we had to create a system to determine just who eats where – a system determined by age. Adults and teenage grandchildren eat at the dining room table while the younger kids have their own less formal gathering in the kitchen. However, when a grandchild turns 13 he has achieved his "rite of passage," and officially graduates from the kitchen to the dining room.

It is a privilege to eat in that room – the place where there's an extra fork next to the plate, a cloth napkin wearing a ring, a festive centrepeice with glowing candles, and two stemmed glasses at each setting for juice and water. And the graduate's first meal in this room is marked by ceremony. He enters slowly with his head held high in his new-found maturity.

However, I suspect not all the kids welcome the change. For one thing, more is expected of them. The use of eating utensils is a given, conversation is kind and thoughtful, and entertaining others with impromptu bodily-sounds is strictly forbidden.

Yes, to eat in the dining room, one has to be different – there has to be a "teen" at the end of his age. But in life not all distinctions are good and hardly any are important. And according to our reading today, when God looks at us, He makes no distinctions at all.

The apostle Peter had just returned to Jerusalem after his visit to the home of Cornelius the Gentile. However, upon his return, we discover not all the believers welcomed him with a smile.

> *"... when Peter arrived back in Jerusalem, some of the Jewish believers criticized him. 'You entered the home of Gentiles and even ate with them!' they said"* (Acts 11:2, 3).

As a Jewish man, Peter had done the unthinkable. He had entered and eaten in an "unclean" home – one that did not observe the customs of the Jewish law. The division between Jew and Gentile was vast, and for Peter to span that gap was unheard of. It is no wonder that his friends in Jerusalem were upset. That is, until Peter told them the rest of the story.

He explained his vision of the sheet and animals of every kind. He told them about the command to "get up, kill and eat." He described the godly man Cornelius and the angelic visit. He also told them about the meeting that was definitely a God-appointment. And best of all, Peter said,

> *"I began telling them the Good News, but just as I was getting started, the Holy Spirit fell on them, just as He fell on us at the beginning. And since God gave these Gentiles the same Gift He gave us when we believed in the Lord Jesus Christ, who was I to argue?"* (Acts 11:15, 17).

Whether to Jew or Gentile, God gave His Spirit freely. He still does today. In our lives some distinctions can't be avoided – like age, or preference in dinner entertainment. And while man may get stuck on labels, in God's eyes we're all the same. There are no age distinctions at His table. No one needs a religious tag to enter God's presence. All we need is an open and honest heart and a willingness to receive the gift of His Son.

Everyone Needs a Redeemer

READ ACTS 11:19-30

A while back our family watched the season finale of the TV show "Survivor." You may know the show – a handful of contestants are abandoned in an isolated land to fend for themselves for 40 days. They make friends; they make enemies; they take tests; and cast votes. In the end, only one survivor remains to collect one million dollars. The episodes are spread out over several weeks. Throughout the show the majestic African countryside was beautifully presented. It was amazing to watch – yawning lions, lumbering giraffes, massive elephants. The animals really brought the country to life. You felt like you were there. It was fun to see, but to be honest, I hadn't watched enough to have an opinion on who should win the title. However, one thing that happened toward the end of the contestants' gruelling challenge definitely grabbed my attention.

In order to help the participants and viewers better relate to the natives of the land, the final three contestants were told they must participate in an ancient native custom with the locals. It was a ritual supposedly to cleanse one of one's sins. The three remaining survivors had to walk through a group of colourfully dressed natives who were waving branches and chanting phrases to scare away unclean spirits. I don't know how long the process lasted but in the end, the three were supposedly freed from all evil and sin. At one point during the show, my nine-year-old asked me, "Mom, did he say they needed to be cleansed from their sins?" I said, "Yes, Honey, he did."

Suddenly the program was no longer just entertaining. It became enlightening. Right there on national TV our children saw for themselves humankind's universal craving for redemption. *Webster's* defines redemption as the act of atoning for, or compensating for. In craving redemption, humanity must also acknowledge a universal need for a

Redeemer.

Although they aren't many, these 11 verses of Acts detail a vital stage in the growth of the early Church, especially in the region surrounding Antioch. When the Church in Jerusalem heard of this explosion of growth, they sent a man named Barnabas to give guidance. In verse 24, he is described as "a good man, full of the Holy Spirit and strong in faith."

As the group's new "pastor," Barnabas witnessed an incredible growth in the congregation. And it didn't take long for him to realize that he needed an "assistant pastor." He called on his faithful friend and minister of the Cross, Saul, soon to be known as Paul, and,

> *"Both of them stayed there with the church for a full year, teaching great numbers of people. (It was there at Antioch that the believers were first called Christians)"* (Acts 11:26b).

Isn't that interesting? It was at this point in history that the word "Christian" was adopted. But why were they called "Christians?" The word "Christian" refers to a follower of "Christ," which literally means "the Messiah, the anointed One, the Redeemer." While the title of "Christian" was first conceived in the city of Antioch, certainly the need for a Redeemer wasn't born there.

The human race has needed a Saviour since the fall of man in the Garden of Eden. From the plains of Africa to the streets of Toronto people are well-aware of their need of a good cleaning on the inside. They need to be saved from their sins. The birth of Christianity simply announced the arrival of the Saviour. His name is Jesus, the Christ.

In craving redemption, humanity must also acknowledge a universal need for a Redeemer.

The Power of Prayer

READ ACTS 12:1-19

In a 1999 *Decision* magazine article, Shirley Dobson, wife of Focus on the Family founder James Dobson, told of a time early in their ministry when Jim was often away from home. Shirley had become accustomed to his absences and said she was never really frightened while he was away – that is, until one night.

It was about 2:00 a.m. and Shirley awoke with a start. She was afraid and didn't know why. For a few minutes, Shirley lay there worrying, finally forcing herself out of bed and onto her knees. "Oh, Lord," she prayed, "I don't know why I'm so frightened. I ask you to watch over our home and protect our family. Send your guardian angel to be with us." She climbed back into bed and soon fell asleep.

The next morning Shirley found out what had happened the night before. A burglar had robbed her next-door neighbour, entered the couple's bedroom while they slept, and stolen money right off the dresser. It happened at about 2:00 a.m. – the exact time Shirley was inspired to pray.

She then wondered about her own home. If the burglar had wanted to break in, the most logical place would have been the bathroom window which was shielded from the neighbours by a hedge. When she went outside to check, Shirley found the screen was bent and the sill was splintered. Someone had indeed tried to break in! The police later told her that the burglar could have easily gotten in. So what had stopped him?

Shirley Dobson is convinced that God protected them through her panicked prayer. Something, or Someone had discouraged the burglar from entering the house.

Prayer really works. Whether quick and panicked or lingering and intercessory, God answers prayer. And that's exactly the lesson Peter learned.

King Herod Agrippa had arrested the apostle Peter, planning to put him on trial at the end of Passover. However, God had other plans. In the middle of the night an angel appeared in Peter's cell and literally led him out of the prison. Peter, still groggy from sleep, wasn't sure what was going on. He thought he was dreaming until he reached the street, totally free and all alone. He then went to a home where the believers frequently met. In fact, they were gathered there that night, praying for Peter's release. Here is what happened:

> *"He knocked at the door in the gate, and a servant girl named Rhoda came to open it. When she recognized Peter's voice, she was so overjoyed that, instead of opening the door, she ran back inside and told everyone, 'Peter is standing at the door!'"* (Acts 12:13, 14).

Now, before we get too upset with Rhoda, notice the reaction of those praying for Peter:

> *"'You're out of your mind,' they said. When she insisted, they decided, 'It must be his angel.' Meanwhile, Peter continued knocking"* (Acts 12:15, 16a).

It *was* a serious moment but you just have to laugh. Peter had prayed. Rhoda had prayed. The people inside had prayed. But when God answered, no one quite believed it. Aren't we that way too? We present our needs to God often doubting that they'll be met.

Whether we know what we're praying for, or like Shirley Dobson, just know we need to pray, our prayers are heard. We just need to rest in the fact that God is listening, and then expect that one way or another, He will answer.

The Proud Will Be Humbled

READ ACTS 12:20-25

Not long ago, my Grade four son was preparing for a big test on times-tables. He spent an entire week going through drills and memorizing numbers. Over breakfast his brother asked him his six-times tables. After school his sister quizzed him on the sevens, and while cooking supper, I drilled him on multiplying by eight and nine. And then came "test day."

We prayed before he caught the bus, and I prayed during the day. When Eric got home from school I immediately asked how he did on the test. He smiled and said, "I'll tell everyone at supper." *That little stinker*, I thought. And so, we waited.

When suppertime finally rolled around Eric slipped away to his backpack and in grand fashion produced a perfect paper. He had gotten all the problems right! Amongst the cheers Eric then proceeded to do a little dance around the kitchen. He was proud of himself, and we were proud of him. Eric had worked hard for the good grade and he deserved to be proud.

Healthy pride. As a parent, I encourage it in my children. As long as it stays "healthy." It's when pride becomes *noxious*, making those around it *nauseous*, that you know that pride is no longer "good for your health." Today's Scripture passage deals with the common human condition of "unhealthy" pride.

Earlier in this chapter we met King Herod Agrippa who was the grandson of Herod the Great and the monarch during this time. He was ruler of one of the most fertile lands, and as this passage points out, he relished his position of authority. In fact, when neighbouring lands found Agrippa to be angry with them, they sent a delegation to the ruler to make peace. Under these circumstances the King's noxious pride finally caught up with him.

> *"When the day arrived, Herod put on his royal robes, sat on his throne, and made a speech to them. The people gave him a great ovation, shouting, 'It is the voice of a god, not of a man!' Instantly, an angel of the Lord struck Herod with a sickness, because he accepted the people's worship instead of giving the glory to God. So he was consumed with worms and died"*
> (Acts 12:21-23).

To be struck down by the almighty was a pretty powerfull consquence for such a common sin. Powerful yes, but not necessarily surprising, especially if you spend any time getting to know the heart of God. Consider this verse in the book of Isaiah regarding God's heart toward the proud.

> *"The Lord Almighty has a day in store for all the proud and lofty, for all that is exalted (and they will be humbled) ..."* (Isaiah 2:12).

The proud will be humbled. That is not just a threat, but a promise. Other verses in God's Word say that "the proud will be punished" (*Proverbs 16:5*), God will "look at every proud man and bring him low" (*Job 40:11*), and "the proud He pays back in full" (*Psalm. 31:23*).

A. W. Tozer once said that "God is looking for men in whose hands His Glory is safe." Those would be hands that accept earned recognition and then freely give it to the only One who truly deserves the glory.

> *God is looking for men in whose hands His Glory is safe.*
>
> *~ A.W. Tozer*

Making Evil Blink

READ ACTS 13:1-13

"Our goal is complete peace of mind for you and your family."

That is the motto of a new company whose name and location I will not share. As you learn more about it, you'll understand why.

Their sole purpose for existence is to fabricate alibis for the spouse who leads a double life. For a hefty fee, this company will establish for you a believable paper trail. It will furnish ticket stubs for the theatre performance you said you were attending and print up dummy invitations to the business events that kept you away from home. It will even hire official sounding receptionists who will intercept phone calls to the false locations where you're supposed to be. All in the name of "peace of mind for you and your family."

It is revolting! It's insulting, offensive and just morally wrong! The nerve of someone to offer deceit and trickery in the name of "peace of mind"! There are times in life when people have to stand up against dishonesty and those who benefit from it. It's as true in our world now as it was 2,000 years ago. And that's what we find in our reading for today.

This passage marks the launching of the travelling ministry of two apostles, Barnabas and Saul, soon to be called Paul.

As an aside, I've always wondered why his name change was important. Although we're not told the reason, we know that the name "Paul" literally means "small or little." Some think he took the name as an act of humility because he no longer wanted to bear the proud name of Saul.

In today's passage we observe a change in the team's ministry focus. After a powerful time of prayer and fasting the Church at Antioch commissioned Barnabas and Saul to be sent forth as missionaries. Led by God's Holy Spirit, this new team, which included the young John Mark, author of the Gospel of Mark, left for the island of Cyprus. Here they met satanic opposition through a sorcerer who had attached himself to the Roman governor of the region and had enjoyed great influence over him. But the governor became curious about the visiting missionaries and:

> *"The governor invited Barnabas and Saul to visit him, for he wanted to hear the Word of God. But ... the sorcerer... interfered and urged the governor to pay no attention ... he was trying to turn the governor away from the Christian faith"* (Acts 13:7, 8).

It's interesting that as soon as the Light of God's Word was revealed, this "messenger of darkness" turned away and tried to turn the governor away as well. Saul regarded such behavior to be more than just insulting and offensive. He saw it as moral perversion:

> *"Then Saul ... filled with the Holy Spirit, looked the sorcerer in the eye and said, 'You son of the devil, full of every sort of trickery and villainy, enemy of all that is good, will you never stop perverting the true ways of the Lord?"* (Acts 13:9, 10).

It's one thing to choose to live in the shadows of deception. It's quite another to encourage someone else to live in it as well. And so Saul stood up to this evil. As he was filled with God's Holy Spirit, Saul not only looked evil in the eye – he made it blink! And we can too. As we allow God's Spirit to completely fill us, we are able not only to stand up to evil, but just as important, to overcome it.

Pardoned

READ ACTS 13:14-43

It was December 6, 1829, and his name was George Wilson. George was an ordinary man who did ordinary things. That is, until one day. On December 6th, 1829, George abandoned his life as a law-abiding citizen and robbed a United States mail carrier. He was caught and in May of 1830 found guilty on six charges, which included robbery of the mail and "putting the life of the driver in jeopardy." Not long after his guilty verdict, George received his sentence: execution by hanging.

Back then, the laws were harsh and they were swift. But the judgment against George outraged his friends. This was his first offense and no one was hurt. Because the judge had set the sentence, they took their case straight to the top. They went to President Andrew Jackson himself. History records that after much deliberation, President Jackson gave George a full pardon. He was no longer condemned to die.

But here the real story begins. You see, George Wilson, freed from his sentence, refused the pardon. He held in his hands a deserved conviction and the President himself offered to replace it with a full acquittal. But George Wilson refused it. The case made national news and went all the way to the Supreme Court. In its landmark ruling, the Court gave this statement,

"A pardon is an act of grace ... The court cannot give the prisoner the benefit of the pardon, unless he claims the benefit of it ... It is a grant to him: it is his property; and he may accept it or not as he pleases." The U. S. Supreme Court.

He chose not to accept it. In the summer of 1830, before a vast crowd, George Wilson was executed by hanging. With the gift of life before him, this guilt-ridden man chose death. What a waste!

But before you write this story off as a random act by a foolish man, consider this: thousands of people every day are doing just that. The Cross of Jesus is a constant reminder of the pardon God offers to man. A pardon that would result in an eternity in the presence of God, rather than separation from Him in hell. The apostle Paul said,

> *"Brothers, listen! In this Man Jesus there is forgiveness of your sins. Everyone who believes in Him is freed from all guilt and declared right with God ..."* (Acts 13:38, 39).

To be freed from all guilt is a universal need. In a recent poll done by *USA Today*, when adults were asked what they felt most guilty about, 34 percent, a *full third*, said they felt guilty but didn't know why. Like George Wilson, the guilt is there, but they would rather die in it than accept a way out. When offered new life through Jesus, they simply refuse the pardon. What a waste! But it doesn't have to be that way. As Paul said in the book of Romans, when we accept this pardon through the work of the Cross,

> *"The Spirit of life in Christ, like a strong wind, has magnificently cleared the air, freeing you from a fated lifetime of brutal tyranny at the hands of sin and death"* (Romans 8:2 *The Message*).

To free for eternity. To save us from our sins. That is what Jesus came to do. That is the message of the Cross and the empty tomb. Without forgiveness through Jesus we are tied to the guilt of our past. Only as we accept His pardon will we ever know the ultimate acquittal of Grace.

> *To free us for eternity and save us from our sins is what Jesus came to do.*

Claim the Prize

READ ACTS 13:44-52

In July 2001, Glen and Gloria Sims, of Sewell, New Jersey, assumed they had a problem. Someone kept phoning them and sending notices in the mail saying they had just won one million dollars. It was getting rather annoying, what with all that junk mail piling up. They hated hanging up on the guy whenever he called but they were smart. They were not about to fall for his little scam. The Sims were sure that if they just gave it a couple of weeks, he would give up. And they were almost right.

Several weeks after the initial contact, an H&R Block spokesman, the company holding the random draw, called the Sims one more time to let them know they were approaching the deadline for accepting the million-dollar prize. He also informed them that the NBC *Today Show* had gotten wind of their refusal to accept, and they would be the feature on an upcoming report.

At that point, Mr. Sims decided to investigate further. A few days later he appeared on the *Today Show* to tell America that he and his wife had finally gone to H & R Block, and had indeed, claimed their million-dollar prize.

You know the old saying, "If it sounds too good to be true, it *usually* is." Maybe *usually*, but not *always*. Sometimes doubting the incredible can not only lead to a suspicious mind, it can leave you out in the cold. And that's exactly the message Paul shared with some Jewish leaders in our reading for today.

Paul and Barnabas had been preaching in the city of Antioch for some time, and their message of God's grace was miraculously changing lives. So widely-accepted was it that on the very next Sabbath, "almost the entire city turned out to hear them preach the word of the Lord" *(Acts 13:44)*. Not surprisingly, this didn't sit well with everyone. Some Jewish leaders couldn't accept the astounding message of God's grace revealed through the death and resurrection of His Son. They verbally assaulted Paul, ridiculing and slandering him before the people. Even against such strong resistance, the apostles did not back down.

> *"Then Paul and Barnabas spoke out boldly and declared, 'It was necessary that this Good News from God be given first to you Jews. But since you have rejected it and judged yourselves unworthy of eternal life – well, we will offer it to Gentiles'"* (Acts 13:46).

For centuries the Jews had been God's chosen people. They were the descendants of Jacob, later called Israel, making the Jewish nation "the children of Israel." They are still a prominent people and special in the eyes of the Lord. In fact, from their seed He brought the Messiah who purchased redemption for all mankind. Here Paul boldly stated that through Jesus, salvation is available not only to the Jews, but to the Gentiles as well. However, the prize of salvation was not claimed by the Jews as a nation, and as a result, all nations are now eligible to receive God's inheritance. Paul explained it like this:

> *"This mystery is that through the Gospel the Gentiles are heirs together with Israel, members together of one body, and sharers together in the promise in Christ Jesus"* (Ephesians 3:6).

The "Gospel," or the "good news" of the Cross is that we are all equal in its shadow. Jew or Gentile, it doesn't matter. The riches of God are free to all who come for cleansing to the Son of God. The important thing is that we claim the prize.

The riches of God are free to all who come for cleansing to the Son of God.

Invisible Evidence

READ ACTS 14:1-20

For some time, Paul and Barnabas had been an official missionary team. They travelled to many cities preaching the good news of God's amazing grace, and for the most part were well received. Through God's Spirit they conducted many miracles which gave them the credibility they needed to be messengers of God. However, it wasn't unusual for a town that had witnessed these divine acts to violently turn on them, causing them to run for their lives.

Such a life wasn't easy, but it was the life of faith to which Paul and Barnabas had been called. Faith, not only in the words they spoke, but more importantly in the "Giver" of those words. Their devotion went deeper than a "cause." It was linked to an intimate relationship with God Himself – knowing Him without ever seeing Him; trusting Him without any proof. This kind of faith propelled the hearts of Paul and Barnabas, and also the heart of a man who had been crippled from birth. Paul first noticed this man while he was preaching. Sitting in the crowd, he was just another spectator among many with obvious needs. But Scripture records something about this man made him stand out to Paul.

> *"He was listening as Paul preached, and Paul noticed him and realized he had faith to be healed"* (Acts 14:9).

In our passage this man had no name, no use of his legs, no means of independence. Some might even argue that he really had no hope for the future. But as he sat and listened to God's Word, he suddenly had faith. And it was unmistakable. Let's find out what happened as a result.

> *"So [Paul] said, loud enough for everyone to hear, 'Up on your feet!' The man was up in a flash – jumped up and walked around as if he'd been walking all his life"* (Acts 14:10 *The Message*).

Miraculously, the man who was crippled from birth suddenly walked. But how? We're told that he was healed through his faith in God's amazing message of grace. Faith! *Webster's* defines it as "belief without proof" – mental assent without physical evidence. But, how does God's Word define faith? Hebrews gives a definition:

> *"What is faith? It is the confident assurance that what we hope for is going to happen. It is the evidence of things we cannot yet see"* (Hebrews 11:1).

According to Scripture, faith is confident assurance in invisible evidence. This may not be too difficult for a *moment*, but how can one build a *life* on faith? Hebrews again has the answer:

> *"We do this by keeping our eyes on Jesus, on Whom our faith depends from start to finish"* (Hebrews 12:2).

Keeping our eyes on Jesus. Like the old hymn goes, "My hope is built on nothing less than Jesus Blood and righteousness." The same is true with our faith. To live a faith-filled life, we must continually look to the only One Who *is* faithful. His name is Jesus.

> *To live a faith-filled life, we must continually look to the only One Who is faithful.*

The Road to Life

READ ACTS 14:21-28

Not long ago I heard a comedian say that in Canada we have four seasons: almost winter, winter, still winter, and construction. How true that is! Around here road construction crews are common, sometimes even in winter. While we have some of the best roads in the world, and we also have some of the longest traffic delays. Traffic jams of "biblical proportions"!

Recently, I came across a study conducted by the U.S. Federal Highway Administration. If we think *we* have it bad, consider the historical facts their research uncovered.

In the U.S. the total length of interstate highway miles is 44,328. That's a lot of miles. But how impressive is it? During the Roman Empire 2000 years ago, the total length of *their* first-class highways exceeded 49,000 miles. The total miles of their secondary roads was almost five times that distance.

The Bible Almanac describes some of what the Roman people went through to build their roads. When constructing an important road, Roman engineers dug a trench the full width of the road and four to five feet deep. The roadbed was then built up with layers of large and small stones, rammed gravel, and even concrete. If the road led into a city, the top layer was often paved with carefully fitted stones 12 inches thick and 18 inches across. They put a lot of effort into building a road, but then the Romans knew, as we do now, that a road is only as strong as the elements that go into making it. What elements make up the road of your life? Where does that road lead? If you are a believer in Christ, Heaven is your ultimate destination. And according to today's reading, your road may be a bumpy one.

As we know, Paul and Barnabas were a missionary team who had been on the road for quite some time. They had preached the good news of the Cross in several cities with encouraging results. Many people had been made right with God through faith in Jesus. They had begun the journey to their heavenly destination, walking hand in hand with God. However, Paul and Barnabas knew it was important for these new believers to begin their journey with an idea of what lay ahead. Therefore,

> *"... They encouraged them to continue in the faith, reminding them that they must enter into the Kingdom of God through many tribulations"* (Acts 14:22).

What a vivid picture for these citizens of the Roman Empire. While the roads that led into their major cities were neatly designed with precisely fitted stones, the road leading into God's kingdom would be anything but smooth. They would enter it "through many tribulations." In fact, Jesus Himself said about this road to life:

> *"But the gateway to life is small, and the road is narrow, and only a few ever find it"* (Matthew 7:14).

Only a few ever find the narrow road to life. Why is that? Could it be the potholes in the road that discourage them? The entrance into God's kingdom isn't lined with precisely fitting stones but with "many tribulations." And the tribulations may cause some to want to take a detour. But for those who remain faithful, God has prepared a final destination that has streets lined with gold. However, to get there we must not only choose the right road, we must also be prepared to endure the potholes.

But for those who remain faithful, God has prepared a final destination that has streets lined with gold.

Straightened Out By Grace

READ ACTS 15:1-21

Over the years, many humorous stories have been told about Peter and the Pearly Gates. While most of these can make you chuckle, I've found only one that makes you think.

A man had died and, you guessed it, found himself just outside the gates of heaven. Of course Peter was there with a clipboard to meet him. Why Peter is standing at the Pearly Gates with a clipboard, I have no idea, but that's how the story goes. Peter said to the man, "Before I can allow you into heaven, you must answer some questions and gain 100 points." The man agreed. Looking down at his clipboard, Peter said, "Tell me something about your life that would get you some points."

"Well," the man said, "I was married to the same woman for 47 years and was a faithful husband and loving father to our children." Peter nodded his head and said, "Good, good. That'll get you a half a point." Oh oh! This was going to be harder than the man thought.

After a few thoughtful seconds he looked up and said, "I know! During the war a bunch of us were in a foxhole when suddenly a hand grenade landed at our feet. Without even thinking I threw myself onto it to save the lives of my buddies. It turned out that the grenade was a dud, but I received a medal for bravery. Surely that's gotta count for something."

Peter looked at his clipboard and nodded, "Yes, that's another half a point." Things weren't going well.

Peter looked at him and said, "There's got to be something you can tell me to get you all those points."

The man was really sweating now. He thought and thought until he finally threw up his hands and said, "This is impossible! The only way I'm going to make it into heaven – is by the grace of God!" Peter smiled as he put down the clipboard and said, "Welcome home!"

While it's meant to be a joke, the story does state a profound truth. Only by God's Grace are any of us welcomed into His Presence. And that's just what Paul was saying in our reading for today.

For centuries, earning God's favour through the Law had been a way of life for the Jewish people. To accept reliance on His grace alone was not an easy change. They had to adjust how they lived and what they taught. And not everyone understood this. Some Jewish believers told non-Jews that in order to be made right with God they must also fulfill the Jewish Law. This prompted a meeting of Church leaders. At the conclusion of the meeting, they reached a decision and announced:

> *"To God, [the Gentiles] are not different from us [the Jews]. When they believed, He made their hearts pure. So now why are you ... putting a heavy load around the necks of the non-Jewish believers? It is a load that neither we nor our ancestors were able to carry. But we believe that we and they too will be saved by the grace of the Lord Jesus"* (Acts 15:8-10 *New Century Version*).

It is only by the Grace of God that we are saved. It's not that we *need* nothing else. It's that there *is* nothing else. D. L. Moody once said, "the Law tells me how crooked I am; His grace comes along and straightens me out." God's grace will never be about anything you can do to earn it. His grace is only about what He has done to give it.

> *"The Law tells me how crooked I am; His grace comes along and straightens me out."*
> *~ D.L. Moody*

When Two Disagree

READ ACTS 15:22-41

A hundred years ago, on March 13, 1904, the countries of Argentina and Chile did something no two countries had ever done. High in the Andes mountains on the border that separates them, they erected a magnificent statue of Jesus. Entitled "Christ of the Andes," the statue stands as a visual reminder of their pledge of peace. On a plaque at its base an inscription reads, "Sooner shall these mountains crumble into dust than Argentines and Chileans break the peace sworn at the feet of Christ the Redeemer."

However, shortly after the statue was unveiled, there arose a problem. The citizens of Chile began to protest that they had been slighted – the statue's back was turned to Chile. Just as tempers flared, a Chilean newspaper-man saved the day. In his popular column, he announced, "The people of Argentina [plainly] need more watching over than do the [citizens of Chili]." This not only satisfied the people, it also made them laugh.

Common human conflict. It can cause division between two peace-loving countries today, just as in it did in the book of Acts between two God-fearing men.

Paul and Barnabas had come to the end of their missionary journey together. They had pursued God's calling and preached His message side-by-side over many long miles. The ministry trip had gone so well that the two men had initially agreed to do it again. That is, until conflict changed the course of events and altered their lives:

> *"After some time Paul said to Barnabas, 'Let's return to each city where we previously preached the Word of the Lord, to see how the new believers are getting along.' Barnabas agreed and wanted to take along John Mark. But Paul disagreed strongly, since John Mark had deserted them in Pamphylia and had not shared in their work. Their disagreement over this was so sharp that they separated ..."* (Acts 15:37-39a).

Common disagreement caused Paul and Barnabas' ministry team to dissolve. Interestingly, this parting of ways did not cause a division in the Church. Even though this disagreement ended their ministry together, it also launched many successful ventures for them individually. Verse 39 says that Barnabas had a great desire to take the Gospel to his own people. Consequently, he took John Mark with him and sailed for his homeland, Cyprus. And tradition tells us that Barnabas had a successful ministry there. It's even said that from Cyprus a tremendous work was carried into North Africa. As far as Paul is concerned, much of the New Testament accounts for the success of his ministry.

Common human conflict. It will eventually die away. But the message of the Cross – that's something worth fighting for!

Common human conflict. It will eventually die away. But the message of the Cross – that's something worth fighting for!

Just Listen

READ ACTS 16:1-15

Mt. Everest is amazing. Located on the border between Tibet and Nepal, and calculated at a height of more than 29,000 feet, this mammoth mass has long been classified as the world's tallest mountain. It is covered with ice and snow year-round, and the temperature at its summit never climbs above freezing. Before the early 1900's, there were no recorded instances of man setting foot on the mountain, and the locals regarded it as a home of the gods. However, that eventually changed and the expeditions began.

Erik Weihenmayer is one of the elite few who has reached the peak of Mt. Everest – a significant feat. But in order to fully appreciate Erik's accomplishment, you must also know a little about him.

You see, Eric Weihenmayer is blind. In a *Time* magazine article from June 2001, we're told that Erik, along with a group of "sighted" climbers, reached the summit of Mt. Everest even though 90 percent of climbers never do. Everest is so difficult to climb that since 1953,165 have died trying. With the added challenge of being sightless, just how did Erik do it?

Erik succeeded in large part by his ability to listen. He listened to the little bell tied to the back of the climber in front of him, so that he would know which direction to go. He listened to the voices of teammates calling back to him, "Death fall two feet to your right!" so he would know in what direction not to go. He listened to the sound of the ice as his pick dug into it, to know whether the ice was safe to cross. And on May 25, 2001, a sightless man named Erik did something most people will never do. He conquered the world's tallest mountain – in large part by listening. Something tells me there's a lesson in that for us. And it's the same lesson we find in our reading for today.

The apostle Paul was now embarking on his second missionary journey, this time with a man named Silas. Beginning in the town of Derbe, the two men covered a lot of ground, but not necessarily the ground they had intended to cover. Verses six and seven tell us why they changed their plans.

> *"Next Paul and Silas travelled through the area of Phrygia and Galatia, because the Holy Spirit had told them not to go into the province of Asia at that time. Then coming to the borders of Mysia, they headed for the province of Bithynia, but again the Spirit of Jesus did not let them go"* (Acts 16:6, 7).

Amazing! To be so in tune with God's Holy Spirit that He actually guides your steps. Like the blind climber of Mt. Everest, your ears are trained on "His bell," and you know what direction to go.

To actually listen to the voice of God. Joan of Arc did. In fact, one instance when someone mocked her saying, "She says she hears God's voice; why *I* don't hear His voice!" Joan quietly replied, "Don't you wish you did?"

To be led by the voice of God is simple. Once you allow Him to be the Leader in your life, all you have to do is listen.

Once you allow Him to be the Leader in your life, all you have to do is listen.

Reality and Make-Believe

READ ACTS 16:16-24

A while back, our family was invited to the home of another family for dinner and a video. After wolfing down our pizza, we all gathered around the TV to watch the Disney family film, *Air Bud*. With all the lights out and only the glow of the screen before us, both families settled in for the heart-warming story of a boy and his dog. We weren't too far into the movie when my then six-year-old son came over and climbed up on my lap. It didn't surprise because we are a "snuggly family." But then the movie reached a climactic moment. For the dog's own good, the boy was trying to get rid of him, shouting to the dog that he didn't love him anymore. It was very moving. It brought a lump to my throat. But for Eric it did far more than that. Suddenly, in the quiet of the dark room, my little boy turned his face into my neck and began sobbing uncontrollably, deep gut-wrenching, heart-breaking sobs. Everyone turned and looked at him as he said, "Why, Mommy? Why is the boy saying that? He loves the dog! He's making the dog sad. What's gonna happen now, Mommy?"

I had never seen the movie, so I had no idea. But the parents of the other family quickly stepped in and told Eric not to worry – that it would all turn out good in the end.

> *Knowing the difference between reality and make-believe can be difficult... even... for some adults.*

Without giving away too much of the movie, I'll just say that at the story's conclusion, everyone was happy – the boy, the dog, and my son.

On the drive home we had a long talk about what's real and what's pretend. Knowing the difference between reality and make-believe can be difficult. And as we'll see in our reading for today, that's even the case for some adults.

In this passage we read that Paul and Silas had reached Philippi, a major city and Roman colony. There several people listened to the reality of God's grace and found salvation through the Cross of Jesus. However, because Philippi was a Roman colony, many there were heavily into Roman idolatry. That's why the presence of a demon-possessed girl was not out of the ordinary. We're told in verse 16 that she was a slave girl and a fortune-teller who earned a lot of money for her masters, but she was also demon-possessed. This title in itself is a study in contradictions of the *real* and the *make-believe*: demons are real; their ability to fore-tell the future is not. However, there was one observation this girl made that was right on target:

> *"She followed along behind [Paul and Silas] shouting, 'These men are servants of the Most High God, and they have come to tell you how to be saved"* (Acts 16:17).

This is one instance where she was absolutely right. The Apostle James tells us that

> *"Even the demons of hell shudder at the presence of Almighty God"* (James 2:19).

The reality of God's presence is unmistakable. He brings peace (Isa. 26:3), clarity (Prov. 3:6) and hope (Lam. 3: 21-22). And regardless if it is declared by a demon-possed fortune-teller or a Spirit-filled apostle, God's power to save is *not* make-believe.

Remember! They're Listening

READ ACTS 16:25-40

As President of the United States, Franklin Roosevelt often endured long receiving lines at the White House. There, visiting dignitaries would have a chance to shake the hands of the President, First Lady, and other Washington notables before being seated for a formal dinner. It's been said that President Roosevelt grudgingly endured this procedure of etiquette, complaining that no one really paid attention to what was said through the smiles. The story goes that one day he decided to experiment. To each person who came down the line and shook his hand, President Roosevelt murmured, "I murdered my grandmother this morning." The guests all responded with phrases like, "Marvellous!" "Keep up the good work." "We're proud of you." "God bless you, Sir."

His experiment proved to be true until he reached the end of the line and greeted the ambassador from Bolivia. As he listened to Roosevelt's announcement, the bewildered ambassador simply leaned over and whispered, "I'm sure she had it coming."

The art of truly listening! For most of us, it is a lost art. We just don't listen well. However, today's reading reveals that as Paul and Silas were at their lowest, those around them were all ears.

Paul and Silas had been thrown into jail for healing a demon-possessed girl. Demonic idolatry and fortune-telling were big business for Romans and their action was not appreciated. A mob quickly formed against them. As a result, they were stripped and severely beaten with wooden rods and thrown into prison.

How would Paul and Silas have felt? They suffered venomous hatred from the mob and a brutal beating for no good reason. How would *you* have felt? Angry? Depressed? Violent? Those all sound like reasonable reactions. Who could blame you? It's only natural to feel that way. But Paul and Silas weren't living in the *natural*. They were filled with God's *supernatural* Spirit. Oswald Chambers once said, "The Spirit of God is always the Spirit of liberty." Liberty – even in a prison cell? Look at the first part of verse 25 to find out the frame of mind of these beaten, imprisoned and Spirit-filled men.

> *"Around midnight, Paul and Silas were praying and singing hymns to God ..."* (Acts 16:25a).

At what could have been their lowest point, these men were praying and singing. Angry? No. Depressed? No. Singing praise to God? Yes! Bloodied and beaten, they were confident in God. Not only that but,

> *"... the other prisoners were listening"* (Acts 16:25b).

Others were listening. The reaction of Paul and Silas to their circumstances was noted by those around them, as was their miraculous deliverance from prison later that night. Charles Swindoll once said, "I am convinced that life is 10 percent what happens to us, and 90 percent how we react to it." It's the same with us. If God's Spirit lives in us, it will show in our responses to life's tough blows. Do these blows knock us to the mat or drive us to our knees? It's something to think over. And while we're considering it, there's something else to remember. Those around us are listening!

"I am convinced that life is 10 percent what happens to us, and 90 percent how we react to it."
~ Charles Swindoll

The March of the Spirit

READ ACTS 17:1-15

Self-centeredness and rivalry make good story topics. The two go hand-in-hand. For example, the month of July was named after Julius Caesar. Not to be outdone, the Emperor Augustus named the following month after himself. The story goes that since his month of August had only thirty days, and the one named after Julius Caesar had 31, Augustus borrowed a day from February and added it to August, making sure that his month was not inferior to that of Julius Caesar. Classic self-centeredness.

And then there's the story of a minister who had stopped by at the kindergarten Sunday School to share with the class about things money can't buy. "It can't buy laughter and it can't buy love," he told them. Emphasizing his point he said, "What would you do if I offered you $1,000 *not* to love your mother and father?" Stunned silence followed. Finally a small voice squeaked, "How much would you give me *not* to love my big sister?" A classic case of rivalry.

In both these stories, the bottom line was self – a formidable foe some Jewish leaders also faced.

Paul and Silas had been travelling the countryside preaching about God's grace when they reached the town of Thessalonica. It was Paul's custom to attend the weekly services held in the synagogue. His "mission field" was among the Jewish people. What better place to reach them than in their own synagogue. On this occasion,

> *"Paul went into the synagogue as he always did, and on each Sabbath day for three weeks, he talked with his fellow Jews about the Scriptures. He explained and proved that the Christ must die and then rise from the dead. He said, 'This Jesus I am telling you about is the*

> *Christ'"* (Acts 17:2, 3 *New Century Version*).

Paul told it like it was, and still is. Jesus is the Christ. He is the only Way man can be redeemed before God. While many Jewish people were persuaded and accepted Jesus as their Messiah, not all did. Destructive, self-centred rivalry got in the way:

> *"But the Jewish leaders were jealous, so they gathered some worthless fellows from the streets to form a mob and start a riot"* (Acts 17:5a).

A large number of people were coming to a deeper understanding of Scripture and responding to God's message of grace. This made these spiritual leaders jealous – exposing their self-centeredness. And we know that a life centred on "self" misses the mark completely.

Ann Landers once said that "at age 20, we worry about what others think of us. At 40, we don't care what they think of us. And at 60, we discover they haven't been thinking of us at all."

To totally let go of self and allow God's Spirit to dictate our actions. It's not easy. But it is the trademark of a *self-less* life. And if we are marked by this quality not only will *people* notice, *God* will notice!

"At age 20, we worry about what others think of us. At 40, we don't care what they think of us. And at 60, we discover they haven't been thinking of us at all."
~ Ann Landers

The Door

READ ACTS 17:16-34

The apostle Paul had just left the town of Berea, literally fleeing for his life to the Greek city of Athens. At that time, Athens was known as the cultural centre of the world. Verse 21 tells us that "all the Athenians as well as the foreigners in Athens seemed to spend all their time discussing the latest ideas." This was a city on the cutting edge.

While waiting for Silas and Timothy to join him, Paul discovered the depths to which Athens was submerged in idolatry, and he was deeply troubled. His convictions spilled out as he debated in the synagogue and spoke daily in the public square. Before long, some of the local, respected philosophers became involved in the debate and brought him before the "Council of Philosophers." We see Paul at his best as he addressed the council:

> *"Men of Athens, I notice that you are very religious, for as I was walking along I saw your many altars. And one of them had this inscription on it – 'To an Unknown God.' You have been worshipping Him without knowing who He is, and now I wish to tell you about Him"* (Acts 17:22, 23).

And he did tell them. He told them that God "made the world and everything in it." He told them that God "Himself gives life and breath to everything, and He satisfies every need there is." Wisely Paul said that it's in Almighty God – their unknown God – that "we live and move and exist." Paul moved them beyond the *unknown* to the *known*. For many of us, that idea can be rather frightening. And that's the message of a story told by an Arab chief.

A spy was captured and sentenced to death by a general in the Persian army. This general had the bizarre custom of giving condemned criminals a choice between the firing squad or "the big, black door." At the time scheduled for the execution, guards brought the spy to the Persian general who said, "What will it be – the firing squad or the big black door?" The spy hesitated for a long time. He finally chose the firing squad. And a few minutes later, the shots rang out. Shaking his head the general turned to his aide and said, "They always prefer the known to the unknown."

Curious, the aide asked, "What lies beyond the big door?"

"It leads to freedom," the general answered. "I've known only a few brave enough to take that door."

And so it is with God. For many today, He is the "great unknown." "I am the door," Jesus said. But out of fear they avoid the only real door to life and freedom that exists. Jesus also said, "if the Son has set you free, you are free indeed" (*John 8:36*). There is freedom in the unknown if you choose God.

Only the brave have the faith to find it.

> *"if the Son has set you free, you are free indeed."* (John 8:36)

Don't Be Afraid

READ ACTS 18:1-17

Former Soviet leader Joseph Stalin was one of the cruelest dictators in history. His tactics were brutal and aggressive and he had no problem with imprisoning and executing his opponents. Upon his death, Nikita Khrushchev, his successor as first secretary, immediately enacted several policy changes. He also openly and harshly criticized his predecessor. Apparently on one occasion, as the new first secretary was condemning Stalin in a public meeting, he was interrupted by a shout from the audience. "You were one of Stalin's colleagues," he said. "Why didn't you stop him?" A hush filled the room as Khrushchev roared, "Who said that?" This led to an agonizing silence. Nobody in the room dared move a muscle, let alone speak. Khrushchev quietly replied, "Now you know why."

Intimidation can scare a person speechless. When faced with aggressive opposition, it's a natural human reaction. And throughout the pages of history, few faced more aggressive opposition than the apostle Paul.

After leaving Athens, Paul moved on to the other major city of the region, Corinth. Corinth was like many major cities today – an affluent, sophisticated, metropolitan centre of about half a million people. To make a living and put food on his table, Paul worked as a tentmaker. While there, he became friends with another Jewish tentmaker and his wife, Aquila and Priscilla, and that is where he lived and worked until the arrival of Silas and Timothy. At that point Paul was then free to devote all his time to spreading the message of Jesus as Messiah.

Unfortunately, many did not accept this message. Shaking their dust from his robe, Paul said to the Jews, "Your blood be upon your own heads – I am innocent. From now on I will go to the Gentiles." And that's just what he did. Verse 8 says that "many Gentiles in Corinth became believers and were baptized." Paul's ministry to them was effective. But we know that as the effectiveness of the message increases, so does the evil that opposes it. And I believe that's precisely why:

> *"One night the Lord spoke to Paul in a vision and told him, 'Don't be afraid! Speak out! Don't be silent! For I am with you, and no one will harm you ..."*
> (Acts 18:9, 10a)

"Don't be afraid! Speak out!" God said. Don't let the aggression of others scare you speechless. At this point in Paul's life, God knew he needed to hear those words. Maybe you need to hear them too. If you do, then keep listening because when it comes to human fear, God's Word has so much more to say. Jesus said, "I am here! Don't be afraid!" (*Matthew 14:27b*). He also said, "...be sure of this: I am with you always..." (*Matthew 28:20b*). In the book of Isaiah, God said, "Don't be afraid, for I am with you ... I will strengthen you. I will help you. I will uphold you ..." (*Isaiah 41:10*). And then in the book of Jeremiah, "Be not afraid ... for I am with you to deliver you" (*Jeremiah 1:8*).

Don't be afraid! Those words are repeated countless times in the Bible. In fact, the phrase, "fear not" is the most repeated command in the New Testament. Don't fear man – trust God. Why?

> *"Be not afraid ... for I am with you to deliver you"* (Jeremiah 1:8).

As we speak out in boldness for Him, we can be certain of this: God will never leave us alone.

Heart Knowledge

READ ACTS 18:18-28

A new pastor desired to really get to know his congregation. Therefore, every Sunday morning he visited a different Sunday School class. His first stop was the Junior Boys. The teacher introduced him to the class and said to him, "Pastor, this morning we're studying Joshua."

"That's wonderful," said the new pastor. "Let's see what you're learning. Who tore down the walls of Jericho?"

Little Johnny shyly raised his hand and whispered, "Pastor, I didn't do it."

Taken aback the pastor asked, "Come on now, who tore down the walls of Jericho?"

The teacher leaned over and said quietly, "Pastor, little Johnny's a good boy. If he says he didn't do it, I believe him."

Flustered, the pastor went to the Sunday School director and related the story to her. The director, looking worried, explained, "Well, sir, we've had some problems with Johnny. Let me talk to him and see what I can find out."

Really bothered by this lack of biblical knowledge, the new pastor approached the deacons and told them the whole story. The group sat in stunned silence. Finally a white-haired gentleman thoughtfully stroked his chin and said, "Pastor, this appears to be bothering you a lot. I propose that instead of making a big deal, we simply take the money from the general fund to pay for the walls, and leave it at that."

A working knowledge of the Bible quite often comes in handy. As demonstrated by the apostle Paul, a clear understanding of God's Word can be the best way to lead others into His amazing grace.

We've followed Paul for some now time as he's travelled through Greece boldly telling about Jesus. In Corinth he befriended Aquila and Priscilla, a Jewish couple that embraced Jesus as Messiah. This couple moved their home and ministry to the city of Ephesus where they met the cultured and eloquent Apollos. In verses 24 and 25, we learn about this man.

> *"Meanwhile, a Jew named Apollos, an eloquent speaker who knew the Scriptures well, had just arrived in Ephesus from Alexandria in Egypt. He had been taught the way of the Lord and talked to others with great enthusiasm ..."* (Acts 18:24, 25a).

Apollos was from Alexandria, a city known for its higher learning. Located in Egypt, it boasted a great university and one of the finest libraries in the world. No doubt Apollos was well versed when it came to a scholastic understanding of the Scriptures. Obviously, he was passionate in sharing that knowledge. However, we're told that only after counsel from Aquila and Priscilla did he fully understand Jesus' mission of grace. With this new "heart-knowledge," Apollos was eager to share the message.

> *"He refuted all the Jews with powerful arguments in public debate. Using the Scriptures, he explained to them, 'The Messiah you are looking for is Jesus'"* (Acts 18:28).

He used the *Scriptures* to prove that Jesus is the Messiah. What I find amazing is that day, the only Scriptures available were those of the Old Testament. Even then, the Messiahship of Jesus could be validated.

Our lives are changed when the knowledge of God's Word moves from our head to our heart. It happens when we receive His Word with understanding. Not only is that the only way to truly know Almighty God – it builds a foundation for introducing Him to others.

Seize the Day

READ ACTS 19:1-10

In his work, *Dealing With Discouragement*, author Bruce Thielemann told this amazing story. After years of working for the postal service, a faithful employee reluctantly reached retirement age. As he sat on his porch waiting for his first Social Security check, he was extremely discouraged. "Is this what my life is going to be from now on" he wondered, "just sitting on the porch waiting for my check to arrive?"

While considered "old" by the government, this man knew he was still very capable. Contemplating life, he made a list. He listed all the things he had going for him – his blessings and capabilities. The list was long. He even included the fact that he was the only person on earth who knew his mother's recipe for fried chicken. It had eleven herbs and spices. Armed with the recipe he went to a nearby restaurant and asked if he could work there cooking the chicken. It quickly became the most popular item on the menu. Soon he opened his own restaurant. And then a string of restaurants. Eventually, Harland Sanders sold the international Kentucky Fried Chicken franchise for a price tag in the millions. And in 1986, KFC was acquired by Pepsico Inc. for an estimated $840 million dollars.

What very well could have been the end of his productiveness was actually the beginning of something great.

It all began with a 65-year-old gentleman and his $105 Social Security check. What a way to seize the day! What could have been the end of his productiveness was actually the beginning of something great. This sounds a lot like the summary of a certain period of time for the apostle Paul.

The 19th chapter of Acts marks the beginning of Paul's third missionary journey. He was in Ephesus introducing the mighty power of God's Holy Spirit to believers.

> *"Then Paul went to the synagogue and preached boldly for the next three months, arguing persuasively about the Kingdom of God"* (Acts 19:8).

During his brief time at the synagogue, Paul had a successful ministry. We're told that by the time he left, he took new believers with him. But if it was going so well there, why did he leave?

He left the synagogue because of malicious opposition. *The Amplified Bible* says they were "hardened and unbelieving, discrediting and ... speaking evil of the Way of the Lord." Paul's ministry in Ephesus however, was far from over, but where could he go? He had a vital message for the city and he needed a central location to give it. And this is where Paul seized the day!

In Ephesus there was a school operated by a man named Tyrannus. Usually it was a very busy place, but in the afternoon there was a two or three hour period while it was empty for the daily siesta. It was perfect! It is believed that this was the time and place where Paul preached the good news of the Cross of Christ for two solid years. Scripture records that

> *"Because of his work, every Jew and Greek in the country of Asia heard the Word of the Lord"*
> (Acts 19:10b *New Century Version*).

Every person in the country heard the Word of the Lord! Paul's ingenuity turned an end into the beginning of a tremendous ministry. Unlike Col. Sanders, Paul's endeavour didn't bring in millions of dollars. But it did something far more valuable. The ministry of Paul ultimately brought in millions of souls.

The Real Thing

READ ACTS 19:11-20

Our family just loves dogs, which is good because we happen to have one – Scotty. But Scotty has a blind spot. He doesn't know he's the family dog. Scotty thinks he's our youngest child who happens to eat off the floor. The truth is, he's just as important to us as he thinks he is. That's why when I came across the "Dog's Code of Conduct" from the Shiloh Ranch of Calder Idaho, I immediately thought of Scotty. Here are a few canine words of wisdom that could easily apply to humans as well:

- Never pass up the opportunity to go for a joyride.
- Run, romp, and play daily.
- When loved ones come home, always run to greet them.
- Take long naps and stretch before rising.
- Avoid biting when a simple growl will do.
- (And my favourite) When someone is having a bad day, be silent, sit close by, and nuzzle them gently.

A loving dog truly can be "man's best friend." Scotty has such a special place in my heart that when I saw a small statue resembling him on sale, I just had to buy it. It makes me think of him. Same bushy eyebrows, same long snout. But there is a major difference. And it's the one that matters most. When you gaze into this dog's eyes, something is missing. No sparkle. No snuggliness. No carefree spirit. While nice to look at, it's just a piece of plaster. It's cold and hard and obviously missing that vital power source – life. It resembles a certain group of people we'll read about today.

The ministry of Paul in the city of Ephesus had really taken off. As we're told in the *Amplified Bible*, for two years he spoke regularly to great crowds so that, "all the inhabitants of [the province] of Asia ... heard the Word of the Lord" (*Acts 19:10*). That's an incredible accomplishment and it was a direct result of Paul's obedience. God's Spirit was operating so powerfully through Paul that he did "unusual and extraordinary miracles" (*Acts 19:11*) – miracles that others not filled with God's Spirit tried their best to imitate. Such was the case with the seven sons of a leading priest who:

> *"tried to use the name of the Lord Jesus to force the evil spirits out. They would say, 'By the same Jesus that Paul talks about, I order you to come out!' ... But ... an evil spirit said to them, 'I know Jesus, and I know about Paul, but who are you?' Then the man who had the evil spirit jumped on them. Because he was so much stronger than all of them, they ran away from the house naked and hurt"* (Acts 19:13b).

What a backlash! They said the right words. They used the name of Jesus. And yet they were pounded senseless. Why?

The answer is hidden in our little plaster Scotty. It may look like the real thing, but it is totally useless without the spark of life – Life in the Spirit of God Who imparts power. Without Him, there is no warmth, no contact, no power.

And so it is with us. It's not enough to go to church and "resemble" one who is plugged in to God. With Him living inside of us we can be charged with the real thing. Then we too can be plugged in to all the potential that comes with His mighty power.

Love Paid the Price

READ ACTS 19:21-41

When our daughter Andrea was little, she was constantly looking for ways to show her love. She brought me handfuls of dandelions, cans full of worms, and even the odd live reptile. And of course with each grand presentation I would hug her tightly and smile, saying it was the best gift she could give. And I gazed into her sparkling five-year-old eyes, I knew it was true.

When you're a child, giving "priceless" gifts is easy. When we grow older however, the media tries to convince us that those gifts must carry a hefty price tag. "Show her your love with diamonds," the ads say. "They are forever." But then again, so are your payments.

That's the cue for an onslaught of commercials from credit card companies. They'll help you express that "love" – over time – with interest.

Those little plastic cards arouse a "love/hate" relationship. We love what they do for us, but we hate what they demand from us. To pay off those cards requires a lot of our time, energy, and focus – much like a relationship with God. Only these little "gods" give nothing in return. In fact, the only thing they offer is more debt. Temporal "gods" made by hands of flesh – idols. They are greedy. They are fleeting. And they are the topic of our reading for today.

Paul had been ministering in Ephesus for quite some time and was planning to leave soon to go to Macedonia. However, before he could leave, serious trouble developed for those sharing the message of the Cross. It began with Demetrius, a silversmith who had a thriving business producing silver shrines for the Greek goddess, Diana. He employed many people. One day he called them all together along with other similar manufacturers in the area, and spoke to them saying:

> *"Gentlemen, you know that our wealth comes from this business. As you have seen and heard, this man Paul has persuaded many people that handmade gods aren't gods at all ..."* (Acts 19:25b, 26a).

I love that verse. What a profound truth this man unwittingly uttered! And what an immense truth for us to remember. "Handmade gods aren't gods at all." They don't deserve our time, our energy, or most importantly, our focus. And yet we give to them – to meet our obligations of course – all the while obligating ourselves even deeper. But we want to "show" our love and this seems to be the only way we can do it. We feed these little "plastic gods"with the labour of our hands and set them high on the throne of our lives. And then we wonder exactly where our lives went off track.

Ann Landers once said that "most of us would be willing to pay as we go, if we could just finish paying for where we've been." It seems we spend our futures in the present paying off the debts of our past. And because there are some things in our past we can never make amends for, we feel forever indebted. But then, in comes the One true God. Just listen to what He did to "show His love."

> *"But here is how God has shown His love for us. While we were still sinners, Christ died for us"* (Romans 5:8 *New International Reader's Version*).

While we were up to our eyebrows in the debts of our past, Jesus died for us. He died for you. But that's not all He did. While He paid the price to release you from the past, He also did something just as important. Three days later He came alive – to give you the power to soar into your future.

His Forever Love

READ ACTS 20:1-12

These days love seems to be expressed everywhere – and the commercial media has no small part to play. It is doing a good job of getting us to bypass our intellect and buy straight from the heart. There's the lottery commercial where adult children buy their parents a new home. And the coffee commercial where the bride-to-be has one last coffee with her dad. Even the slogan for one of the major fast food chains encourages us to "love" it.

Declarations of love are on our own lips. We love the weather or someone's new shoes! And there are some who have been creative enough to share their announcement of true love with millions – as did the soldier who proposed marriage during the Superbowl. Just about everyone is saying, "I love you" to that special someone. In some cases, unfortunately, they are saying it to many "special someones" at the same time!

However, that was not the case with my "special someone." During his teen years, Ron's mother, Norma-Jean, had encouraged him never to tell a girl he loved her unless he was going to marry her. That is pretty good advice in our "love-slinging" world. And so, when Ron and I started dating, it seemed only natural that our conversation would include this advice from his Mother. And although I had never met her, I already liked her.

Ron and I dated for quite some time – well over a year – when he developed a sudden case of "cold feet." Actually, he dropped me cold! And in the process, he broke my heart.

We were in university at the time and seeing him daily didn't help. We had classes together, meals together, and we even studied together. During this time we became best friends, without the attachment that comes with dating. This went on for seven months, and over time my heart mended, although I had become much more cautious. Finally after a summer apart, Ron came back with a sharpened focus on both school and me. One warm summer evening, with a humble heart, Ron asked me to take him back. But I wasn't easily persuaded. Actually, I was terrified – afraid that we would start dating and Ron's feet would once again turn cold. I didn't want to give him my heart, only to have him, without warning, give it back again. And I told him so.

To be honest, I had expected Ron to grovel a bit. The thought crossed my mind that he deserved it after all I had been through. But instead, he took me by surprise. I saw in his eyes a new and steady determination. He spoke with confidence, and said something I had never heard him say before. Something that I knew was reserved for only one person in his life. Looking deeply into my eyes, Ron said to me, "You don't have to worry about me leaving ever again because ... I love you."

I love you! I knew just what that meant. Those three words spoke volumes to me. They were Ron's pledge of undying devotion. His eternal commitment of his "forever" love. Three little words that I still love to hear! Sometimes love can be conveyed in one brief sentence, or as when the apostle Paul spoke of God's love, sometimes it can take all night.

As usual, today's portion of Acts finds Paul preaching. What may have been unusual, was that he appeared to have preached all night. Paul spoke of the matchless love of God in sending His Son to earth; of the incredible love that drove Jesus to the Cross; of the powerful love that propelled Him on the third day from the grave. Paul spoke of God's amazing Grace that reached down to sinful man to draw him close. All for no other reason than love. God's undying devotion; His eternal commitment; His *forever love*. And if it takes all night to convey it, then all I've got to say is, "Paul, talk on!"

Complete Surrender

READ ACTS 20:13-38

The movie *Chariots of Fire* is based on the real life story of a man named Eric Liddell. Eric was born in 1902 to missionary parents in China and was schooled in London. His family home was in Edinburgh, Scotland.

Eric was a spiritually grounded young man who had a strong and devout faith in Christ. The headmaster at his school remarked that "he was a boy entirely without vanity." He was also an extremely talented runner. His missionary father encouraged him to "run in God's name, and let the world stand back and wonder." His style, while successful, was definitely unique. One author wrote, "Liddell ran with abandon, head tilted toward the skies, knees thrust upward to his chin, feet rising high from the ground." Eric didn't focus on style; he just "ran with abandon." And at the 1924 Olympics in Paris Eric ran right onto the pages of history.

En route to the Paris Olympics Eric learned that in order to compete in the 100-metre dash, the race he was favoured to win, he would have to run the qualifying heats on a Sunday. But he considered Sunday the Lord's Day and he refused to do it. At a reception in Paris, the Scottish nobility tried their best to persuade the runner to change his mind, but he was steadfast. He would not run on a Sunday, and so did something unheard of in the Olympic games – he voluntarily forfeited his best chance for a gold medal. Eric then prepared to compete in the 400-metre, an event he had not trained for and was not favoured to win. But to everyone's complete astonishment, Eric Liddell came in first, won the gold medal, and set a new world record. He finished five metres ahead of the second place runner.

"The Flying Scotsman," as he came to be known, *walked off* of one race and *ran off* with another. All with "total abandon." After the Olympics he went to China where he married and started a family. Sadly, at the young age of 43, after being interned in a Chinese prison camp, Eric Liddell, Olympic gold medalist and missionary to China, died of a tumour in his brain. As his life was slipping away Eric lifted his eyes toward Heaven and said, "It's complete surrender."

Total abandon. Complete surrender. There is no better description of a life committed to God. Such was also the life of the apostle Paul.

While in Ephesus, Paul shared his heart with a group of believers. A devout man, totally abandoned to the will of God, Paul said that he was "irresistibly drawn by the Holy Spirit" to live his life in surrender to God. This passage is a beautiful example of the true heart of the apostle Paul:

> *"But my life is worth nothing unless I use it for doing the work assigned me by the Lord Jesus – the work of telling others the Good News about God's wonderful kindness and love"* (Acts 20:24).

Paul "followed hard after God" (*Psalm 63:8 KJV*). Like Eric Liddell, the race was laid out before him, and he ran it with abandon. Missionary and martyr Jim Elliot once said, "One does not surrender a life in an instant. That which is lifelong can only be surrendered in a lifetime." A lifetime of commitment and faithfulness. But most important, a lifetime of *complete surrender* to God.

> *"One does not surrender a life in an instant. That which is lifelong can only be surrendered in a lifetime."*
> *~ Jim Elliot*

The Lord's Will Be Done

READ ACTS 21:1-14

Good advice. It is something we can all use. But too often when we get it, few of use it. It's been said that the trouble with good advice is that it usually interferes with our plans. Recently I came across some bits of advice from one of my favourite authors, Max Lucado. They're from his book, *In the Eye of the Storm*. Listen closely and see if you can find some words of wisdom to hold onto.

- "Love God more than you fear hell."
- "Once a week, let a child take you on a walk."
- "Make major decisions in a cemetery."
- "Succeed at home first."
- "Listen twice as much as you speak, and pray twice as much as you fret."
- And my favourite, "When you can't trace God's hand, trust His heart."

These are good bits of advice, especially about trusting God. But for some of us, recognizing the *need to take advice* is not as difficult as recognizing the *need to stop giving it*. We want to share our wisdom even when that wisdom is unwanted. We pray and advise all to no avail; our advice is not taken. But could it be we use the cover of giving advice to mask our lack of trust in God? If this sounds a little like you, don't fret. It also sounds like some believers in the apostle Paul's company.

Paul had been travelling extensively, sharing the good news of God's grace. He appeared inexhaustible in his desire to tell as many people as possible about the Cross of Christ, and he was highly respected for this. However, there came a time when those who cared about Paul were quite outspoken about their fear for his safety. They had great apprehension over Paul's impending journey to Jerusalem. Several of them advised him not to go.

> *"We ... found the local believers, and stayed with them a week. These disciples prophesied through the Holy Spirit that Paul should not go on to Jerusalem ..."* (Acts 21:4).

Also:

> *"... we who were travelling with him, as well as the local believers, begged Paul not to go on to Jerusalem"* (Acts 21:12).

His friends felt so strongly, that they literally begged Paul not to go. They gave him the best advice possible and yet Paul still refused it. It must have been extremely frustrating for them. What could they do? What would you have done? They said:

> *"When it was clear that we couldn't persuade him, we gave up and said, 'The will of the Lord be done'"* (Acts 21:14).

They gave in – finally – to the will of God! Sometimes the most difficult task in life is to relinquish someone you love to God's perfect care. But because of trust, you know that this is the most loving thing you can do.

Common Ground

READ ACTS 21:15-26

Against the wishes of believers from various regions, the apostle Paul proceeded to Jerusalem. There he received a warm welcome from the Jerusalem Church, and also a fair warning. The large congregation of Jewish believers in the city were a little put out with Paul. They had heard incriminating reports that Paul was preaching against their traditional customs, literally encouraging new Jewish believers to forsake the Jewish law. However, this was not true. In fact, in his first letter to the Church in Corinth, Paul stated,

> *"Each one should retain the place in life that the Lord assigned to him and to which God has called him ... Keeping God's commands is what counts"*
> (1 Corinthians 7:17, 19b *NIV*).

Paul was a firm believer in the unity of the Church. For this reason he preached that the freedom of God's grace permeated the confines of the Jewish law. Grace, he taught, was available to both the average Gentile and the faithful Jew. No damage was done if a person remained in the Jewish system. Damage resulted from trusting in that system for salvation. While preaching these truths, Paul still had to dispel the false rumours. And to do this the Jerusalem believers communicated their plan:

> *"Four of our men have made a promise to God. Take these men with you and share in their cleansing ceremony. Pay their expenses so they can shave their heads. Then it will prove to everyone that what they have heard about you is not true ..."*
> (Acts 21:23 *New Century Version*).

Paul was an educated Jewish man who had been freed from his legalistic past. Yet, in order to bring unity, he willingly complied with their request. Thomas Jefferson once said, "In matters of style, swim with the current; in matters of principle, stand like a rock." In effect, this is just what Paul did. And he did it more than once. He stated,

> *"Even though I am free of the demands and expectations of everyone, I have voluntarily become a servant to any and all in order to reach a wide range of people ...I didn't take on their way of life. I kept my bearings in Christ ... [all this] in my attempts to lead those I meet into a God-saved life"*
> (1 Corinthians 9:19-23 *The Message*).

What an amazing example of selfless love! God grant us to set aside our own pursuits and be consumed with the pursuits of God; to share the message of God's grace in as many ways as possible. May we too be like Paul and "find common ground with everyone so that [we] might bring them to Christ" (*Acts 21:22*).

> *"Find common ground with everyone so that [we] might bring them to Christ."*
> *~ (Acts 21:22)*

Standing Firm for God

READ ACTS 21:27-40

I love classic television. One of my all-time favourites is *The Andy Griffith Show*. I love the happy endings, like the time Opie was being tormented by a bully. With a little patience and a lot of wisdom, his father Andy encouraged him to overcome his fears and to stand up to the bully. Opie did, and sported a pretty good shiner to prove it.

They are cute stories with happy endings. But real life – now that's another story. For instance, consider the disciples of Jesus. If anyone could write a gripping story about being bullied, these guys could. And it would be true. While much of what they endured is recorded in the pages of Scripture, quite often for the end of their life-stories, we must look to tradition. Tradition tells us that:

- John fared the best – he died of extreme old age.
- Judas Iscariot, after betraying his Lord, hanged himself.
- Peter was crucified head down during the persecutions of Nero.
- Andrew died on a cross in a Grecian colony.
- James the younger brother of Jesus was thrown from a pinnacle of the Temple, and then beaten to death with a club.
- James the son of Zebedee was beheaded in Jerusalem.
- Matthew was violently killed with an ax in North Africa.
- Thomas the doubter was run through with a lance in the East Indies.
- Philip was hanged against a pillar at Herapolis.
- Thaddeus was shot to death with arrows.
- Simon died on a cross in Persia.
- And Bartholomew found his end in Armenia, where he was flayed alive (literally had his skin ripped from his body).

What would have driven these incredible men to stand by their Saviour and follow Him all the way to such gruelling deaths? Surely if the story of Jesus was not true, they would have abandoned the charade long before then. But these men ate with Jesus, lived with Him and prayed with Him. They *saw* the blind see, and *danced* with the leaping lame. These were not stories they had *heard.* They were experiences they had *lived.* And I would imagine no experience was more vivid in their memories than that first sight of their risen Lord. Jesus, whom they saw die, now alive – the risen Saviour; the Messiah. And it was this steadfast claim that drove these men to endure more severe persecution than anyone could imagine. Anyone that is, except maybe the apostle Paul.

Paul was in Jerusalem, a city on the brink of one of the world's most vicious periods of religious persecution. His friends begged him not to go, and warned him that danger awaited. But he went anyway and walked right into a hornets' nest of hatred. A crowd formed against him and beat him, trying to kill him. And as was predicted, Paul was arrested. You can't help wondering if the arrival of the soldiers might not have been a welcome sight to Paul because,

> *"... the mob grew so violent the soldiers had to lift Paul to their shoulders to protect him. And the crowd followed behind shouting, 'Kill him, kill him!'"*
> (Acts 21:35, 36).

Paul faced intense hatred such as this on a regular basis because of his stand for Christ. A stand that would eventually it cost him his life.

It's been said that "if you don't stand for something, you'll fall for anything." That's one more good reason to keep standing firm for God.

Straight Talk

READ ACTS 22:1-16

A lot has been said lately about the way things are said. "Politically correct" is a term that now not only applies to government but to everyday citizens as well. It seems everyone is climbing on board the "walk-on-eggshells" bandwagon, maybe even some churches. I recently came across someone's idea of "politically correct" adjustments to a few old favourite hymns. What would you think if you opened your hymnal and found titles like these?

- "A Comfy Mattress Is Our God"
- "Joyful, Joyful, We Kinda Like Thee"
- "Above Average Is Thy Faithfulness"
- "Blest Be The Tie That Doesn't Cramp My Style"
- "He's Quite A Bit To Me"
- "Pillow Of Ages, Fluffed For Me"
- "What An Acquaintance We Have In Jesus"

And then there is the ever popular two-some:

- "I Surrender Some"
- "Take My Life and LET ME BE"

The language of our day is not only becoming more ambiguous – spiritually speaking it's becoming dangerous. We need to get back to telling it like it is. We need to talk straight. We need to become more like the apostle Paul.

Paul had arrived in Jerusalem – a diverse city with several cultures. A crowd, certain that Paul was speaking against their culture, had assembled against him causing him to be arrested. To clear the air, Paul said to the hostile crowd,

> *"'Brothers and esteemed fathers,' Paul said, 'listen to me as I offer my defense.' When they heard him speaking in their own language, the silence was even greater"* (Acts 22:1, 2).

Paul was deemed a stranger and an outsider, yet when he stood to deliver his message, he spoke in their language. A "seeker friendly" approach many churches today have applied well. He got their attention by using this fresh approach, and then delivered the timeless message of God's grace.

We can learn so much from Paul. We need to be bold and tactful while never compromising the message. This is an important truth because in the end everyone who has ever lived will have to deal with God's message. According to *The Message Bible*,

> *"God means what He says. What He says goes. His powerful Word is sharp as a surgeon's scalpel, cutting through everything, whether doubt or defense, laying us open to listen and obey. Nothing and no one is impervious to God's Word. We can't get away from it – no matter what"* (Hebrews 4:12, 13).

There is a great need for straight talk. We must have such a desire for people to know God's grace that we are willing to learn their language to tell them. The passion for the message of life must motivate us so much that we are willing to give up our own just to share it.

To do these things is not just to practice the teachings of Paul. It is to follow the example of Jesus.

The Rights of a Citizen

READ ACTS 22:17-30

In Jerusalem Paul was arrested under false charges of defiling the Jewish temple. A mob had formed against him, dragging him out of the temple with full intentions of killing him. When word reached the commander of the Roman regiment that "all of Jerusalem was in an uproar" (*Acts 22:31*), he led his troops to break up the violence. After arresting Paul, he ordered him to be "lashed with whips to make him confess his crime" (*Acts 22:24*). Before his lashing however, Paul said something that probably made the blood of the men in charge run cold:

> *"As they tied Paul down to lash him, Paul said to the officer standing there, 'Is it legal for you to whip a Roman citizen who hasn't even been tried?'"*
> (Acts 22:25).

Paul was a Roman citizen, and this changed everything. The soldiers knew the high value placed on the rights and privileges of a Roman citizen. In fact, an ancient oration contains the words, "It is a crime to bind a Roman citizen, but an unpardonable one to beat him." As a citizen of Rome, Paul was entitled to the privilege of esteemed protection, and his claim was not taken lightly.

> *"So the commandant came and said to [Paul], 'Tell me, are you a Roman citizen?' And he said, 'Yes [indeed]! ... I was born Roman'"*
> (Acts 22:27, 28b *The Amplified Bible*).

Many believe Paul carried something on his person that would have proven his claim of citizenship because the commander took action.

> *"The next day, the commander freed Paul from his chains"* (Acts 22:30a).

His identification as a Roman citizen afforded him certain rights. He still had to stand trial, but he no longer stood alone. Paul now had the entire Roman government standing behind him.

Citizenship has its benefits. Like Paul, we too were once bound in chains. We stood condemned by our lack of credentials. But the Blood of Jesus changed that. Paul says of the power of the Blood:

> *"Remember that in the past you were without Christ. You were not citizens ... you had no hope, and you did not know God. But now in Christ Jesus, you who were far away from God are brought near through the blood of Christ's death. Now you ... are not foreigners ... any longer, but are citizens together with God's holy people. You belong to God's family"* (Ephesians 2:12, 13, 19 *New Century Version*).

Because of the Blood of Jesus we belong to God's family and enjoy its unmerited privileges. His Blood allows us to live our lives under the eternal protection to which a citizen of God's kingdom is entitled.

This isn't a freedom into which we are born. It is a freedom we acquire when we are "born again."

> *Because of the Blood of Jesus we belong to God's family and enjoy its unmerited privileges.*

The Hope of Resurrection

READ ACTS 23:1-11

The apostle Paul was in Jerusalem, on trial before the Sanhedrin, which is the Jewish high council. This group of religious leaders included two of the main Jewish sects, the Pharisees and the Sadducees. Because of the variance in their interpretation of Scripture, there were many differences between these highly educated groups. And they often discussed these differences publicly and passionately. But perhaps no other topic spurned their anger more than that of resurrection. The Pharisees believed in resurrection whole-heartedly, while the Sadducees were certain it wasn't true. However, the two groups had one thing in common – their mutual revulsion at Paul and his stand for Christ. Paul was a rebel and a reformer who preached redemption not based on the law. This bred venomous hatred. Many times they united against him, both verbally and physically. They even instigated a mob to try and kill him. Again Paul stood face to face with seething anger. What would he say? To begin with, Paul courageously spoke his heart:

> *"Paul surveyed the members of the council with a steady gaze, and then said his piece: 'Friends, I've lived with a clear conscience before God all my life, up to this very moment'"* (Acts 23:1 The Message).

Paul's bold claim of innocence only fuelled the fire of their hatred. As the intensity of hatred directed at Paul grew by the second, he had a flash of inspiration.

> *"Paul realized that some members of the high council were Sadducees and some were Pharisees, so he shouted, 'Brothers, I am a Pharisee, as were all my ancestors! And I am on trial because my hope is in the resur-*

rection of the dead!" (Acts 23:6).

Paul's brilliant insight immediately changed the tone of the trial and turned their hate away from himself and onto each other. It may appear that Paul was being a little less than honest, but he wasn't. While he had been brought up as a staunchly legalistic Pharisee, he now was free through Christ. His hope lay not only in the Cross of Jesus, but also in His mighty resurrection afterwards. By dying for our sins and coming to life again, Jesus became not only our Sacrificial Lamb, but our conquering Lion. The apostle John encourages us, saying,

> *"Stop weeping! See, the Lion of the tribe of Judah, the Root (Source) of David, has won (has overcome and conquered)!"* (Revelation 5:5 *The Amplified Bible*).

This was Paul's great hope. The powerful resurrection of Jesus conquered death not just once, but for all time. That is our living, breathing assurance. Our physical end is actually our eternal beginning. Paul staked his life on it. And through God's mighty power we can too.

By dying for our sins and coming to life again, our precious Saviour became not only our Sacrificial Lamb, but our conquering Lion.

Our Light in Darkness

READ ACTS 23:12-35

Not long ago, a mother had taken her two young sons shopping at the mall. Not realizing they had added a new word to their vocabulary, she was shocked when she heard them, in a fit of anger, yell back and forth "I hate you!" and "I hate you too!" Thinking quickly, she calmly interrupted, "That's not very nice," she said. "I'm certainly not going to take two little boys who hate each other to McDonald's for lunch." Her tactic worked and her five-year-old quickly backed down saying, "I don't really hate you, Billy." However, her bubble burst as Billy, with the clear logic of a three-year-old responded, "I still hate you! I'm not hungry."

What do you do with a hatred that knows no bounds – except that of its appetite? But what if one has an "appetite" for hatred? Hatred that can never be quenched until it is fulfilled is dangerous. That's the kind of hatred Paul faced in our reading for today.

It's at the beginning of this text we witness the insatiable appetite of bitter hatred. Looking into the *Message Bible*, let's discover just what their loathing led a group of men to do.

> *"Next day the Jews worked up a plot against Paul. They took a solemn oath that they would neither eat nor drink until they had killed him. Over forty of them ritually bound themselves to this murder pact ..."* (Acts 23:12, 13 *The Message*).

These men who swore an oath denying themselves food until Paul was dead considered themselves "religious." Who was the head of *that* religion? Author Anne Lamott once said that, "You can safely assume you've created God in your own image when it turns out that God hates all the same people you do."

The god of dark hatred bears no resemblance to the "Father of Light." The responsibility is ours to distinguish between the two. The prophet Isaiah said:

> *"Destruction is certain for those who say that evil is good and good is evil; that dark is light and light is dark ..."* (Isaiah 5:20).

Just as a room cannot be light and dark at the same time, so it is with a heart. It cannot yield to darkness while expecting guidance from the Light. But left to ourselves, that's what we do. We're all born into the shadows of a dark world. We all desperately need the illumination of divine Light. So, where is the hope? Perhaps King David described hope the best with these words:

> *"Lord, You have brought light to my life; my God, You light up my darkness"* (Psalm 18:28).

The *NIV* says the Lord "*keeps* my lamp burning." And *The Message* Bible says, "God, you floodlight my life." To be so totally full of the light of God's love that hatred has no place in our hearts. That is our victory over darkness. And in essence, therein lies our hope.

> *To be so totally full of the light of God's love that hatred has no place in our hearts. That is our victory over darkness.*

A Clear Conscience

READ ACTS 24:1-16

The apostle Paul was in Caesarea on trial before Governor Felix. His accusers travelled a long distance to level their false charges against him claiming that he was guilty of inciting riots, planning rebellions, and defiling the Jewish Temple. Of course, none of this was true. And finally it was Paul's turn to speak. Starting in verse 15, here is the beginning of his official rebuttal:

> *"I have hope in God ... Because of this, I always try to maintain a clear conscience before God and everyone else"* (Acts 24:15a, 16).

He first proclaimed his clear conscience. That's quite an accomplishment, to maintain a clear conscience. None of us can do it without divine help. And perhaps no one knows this better than one who struggles with conscience, in this case a woman named Sarah.

Sarah lived in the 1800's, and by any era's standards, she was very rich. Not only was her income a thousand dollars a day – she had inherited twenty million dollars. Today, she would be considered a billionaire. By all outward appearances, Sarah lived the good life. She was well-known in high society and was invited to every social event. She had power. Her name alone opened many opportunities. But her wealth didn't give her peace. Sarah had it all – including heartache.

Her only child had died as an infant, and a short time later tuberculosis took her husband. Overcome with grief and an inherited sense of guilt, Sarah moved her life from the east coast to the west. In San Jose, California, she purchased a small farmhouse with some adjoining acreage and began her quest for peace. What started as a renovation on an old home, quickly turned into employment for 16 full-time carpenters who worked every day, 24 hours a day, for the next 38 years.

The floor plan of this evolving house was bizarre. Hallways leading nowhere were put in at random. A set of stairs leads to the ceiling, and a door opens to a blank wall. The house, which still stands as a tourist attraction, covers six acres, has six kitchens, 13 bathrooms, 40 stairways, 10,000 windows, and 160 rooms.

What would cause a person to be so eccentric and driven? Perhaps at least part of the answer lies in knowing Sarah's full identity. Sarah's last name was "Winchester," of the famed "Winchester repeating rifle." This invention brought millions of dollars to the Winchester family, but death to thousands of others – soldiers fighting on the field of battle; natives standing to defend their land; even young children suffering at the hands of unbridled anger. Sarah's guilt mounted with every rifle sold until finally she could take it no longer. In her agony she tried to atone for the deaths of so many. Sarah built the house with the desire that it be occupied by the spirits of those who had died. By giving her life to this venture, Sarah lost her mind.

Sarah's life illustrates the fact that the human pursuit of a "clear conscience" is never-ending. And without divine intervention, we're not that different from Sarah. Without God we build a life with no purpose and no reason. Paul knew what it was like to have a clear conscience before God. He said:

> *"So now there is no condemnation for those who belong to Christ Jesus. For the power of the life-giving Spirit has freed you through Christ Jesus from the power of sin that leads to death"* (Romans 8:1, 2).

A conscience that's freed from its guilty past results in a life not shadowed by condemnation. How? Through the powerful life-giving Spirit of God. He wants to give that same freedom to you. Leave the past behind and move forward into new life with Him.

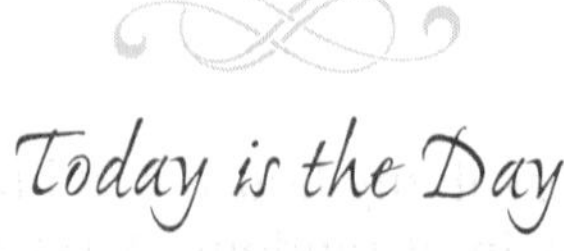

Today is the Day

READ ACTS 24:17-27

After being transported to Caesarea, the apostle Paul stood trial before Governor Felix. While the Scriptures are limited in their description of him, one Roman historian said this concerning Felix: "Through all cruelty and licentiousness he exercised the authority of a king with the spirit of a slave."

While impoverished in spirit, he was wealthy in power. And Paul's accusers knew this. After they stated their case to the Governor against him, it was Paul's turn to speak. He said he was a follower of "the Way," the name given to those who followed the "Way of the Cross." Paul said that he worshiped the God of their ancestors and that his hope was fixed in God alone. Paul exhibited such certainty and boldness that he struck a cord in Felix to the degree that later Felix and his wife requested a private audience with Paul.

> *"As [Paul] reasoned with them about righteousness and self-control and the judgment to come, Felix was terrified. 'Go away for now,' he replied. 'When it is more convenient, I'll call for you again'"* (Acts 24:25).

Felix was compelled to know more about Jesus, but when Paul's teaching hit a little too close to home, he backed out. "I'll call you back some time in the future," he told Paul. But there is no record of Felix ever finding a future with God. Author Denis Waitley says, "there is no such thing as a 'future' decision. You face only 'present' decisions that will affect what will happen in the future." And putting off the most important decision of your life is indeed dangerous procrastination.

Author William Tidwell tells a story of a minister who had a dream. In this dream, Satan and his cohorts were devising effective ways to lure souls to hell. One dark spirit spoke and said, "I know. I will tell the people there is no God." But Satan said, "That will not do, for only fools deny that fact."

Then another fiend of unusual intelligence stood and said, "I will go and tell them that there is nothing to religion, that it's all a farce." But Satan replied, "That will never do, for multitudes have witnessed the progress made by men and women who discover a faith on which to build their lives."

One after another the demons made devious suggestions, but Satan refused them all. Finally, exhausted from the effort, all in the room grew silent. Then the most subtle of all present arose and said, "I know just what to do. I will go and tell them that there is a God, that the Bible is true, and that salvation is real. And then I will constantly remind them that – there is plenty of time."

Plenty of time – "time to make things right with my family;" or, "time to get down to business with God." Of all the tools in his arsenal, perhaps this is Satan's most effective. But it doesn't have to be. Reading from his second letter to the Corinthians, Paul said that:

> "*God is ready to help you right* now. Today *is the day of salvation*" (2 Corinthians 6:2).

Now is the time to make a decision. *Today* is the day to accept the Lord.

It's been said that the tragedy of life is not that it ends so soon, but that we wait so long to begin it.

Don't wait! Choose new life through Jesus today. Don't put off for one more minute that which will determine your eternity.

He Is There

READ ACTS 25:1-27

Paul was still in prison in Caesarea, the same place he'd spent the last two years. Governor Felix eventually left office and was succeeded by a man named Festus. And while Festus looked into Paul's case right away, we can't help but wonder if he too was more concerned about its political ramifications than the discovery of the truth. This became evident when, in an open forum, Festus asked Paul if he'd be willing to go to Jerusalem to stand trial. The Governor knew that by providing this opportunity, he would score big points with the Jewish leaders. He didn't care about Paul. He only cared about his own political future. Paul knew this and countered:

> *"If I've committed a crime and deserve death, name the day. I can face it. But if there's nothing to their accusations – and you know there isn't – nobody can force me to go along with their nonsense ..."* (Acts 25:11 *The Message*).

Paul, surrounded by darkness, even then was a fearless man of God. Where did he get his boldness? Certainly you wouldn't expect his circumstances to breed fearlessness. So what was Paul's secret? Perhaps Paul clung to the same source of courage as did a certain little boy who found himself in darkness.

Author Kenneth Wilson tells the story of growing up in the hills around Pittsburgh. His childhood home was on one of those hills, three stories high in the front, and four stories in the back. The cellar was at the lowest level and at the top floor was a finished attic complete with two bedrooms, a hallway, and a musty storage room. His family slept in the attic because they found it necessary to rent out the second floor to help pay the rent. Kenneth remembers that as the youngest he was the first one put to bed every night in that attic of dark bedrooms. The walk up the creaky steps was long, and it led into total darkness because the electricity only reached to the second floor. Only a gas light illuminated Kenneth's room and it had to be extinguished once he was settled. He later wrote, "that bed in that room on the third floor seemed to be at the end of the earth, remote from human habitation, close to unexplained noises and dark secrets." Kenneth went on to say that he dreaded the moment the light went out and all he could hear was the sound of his father's footsteps growing fainter on the stairs. "I'll never forget one night," he reflected, "when my father said to me, 'Would you rather I leave the light on and go downstairs, or turn the light out and stay with you for awhile?'" What a question! Light was what he wanted most in that attic bedroom, but when given the opportunity to be near his father, little Kenneth didn't think twice. Eagerly this terrified little boy chose his father's presence in darkness over his absence in light.

Isn't that what we all want – the assurance that someone is there? Just as having his father close by gave this little boy a sense of peace, knowing God was with him gave the apostle Paul incredible courage.

What about you? Are you longing for peace? Do you desperately need courage? Then know this: No matter how dark your world may appear, your heavenly Father is right there beside you. And He's not going anywhere.

No matter how dark your world may appear, your heavenly Father is right there beside you. And He's not going anywhere.

Good News; Bad News

READ ACTS 26:1-11

Things aren't always as they first appear. How often have we been on the receiving end of a flowery compliment, only to then be poked by thorns that show up in the word "but"? Like, "Your new dress is beautiful! *but* did the store run out of your size?" Or, "Your new haircut looks great! *but* don't worry, it'll grow!" And the same thing goes for "good news." Has anyone said to you, "I have good news!" only then to break the "bad news?" According to author James Berkley, such disappointments can become a way of life, especially for some overworked pastors. Here are some humbling comments to pastors from his collection:

- *The good news*: The church board accepted your job description just the way you wrote it.
  The bad news: They formed a search committee to find someone capable of filling it.

- *The good news*: The Women's Association voted to send you a get-well card.
  The bad news: It passed 31 to 30.

- *The good news*: The children's softball team won their first game.
  The bad news: It was against the men's softball team.

And one more for the poor pastor.

- *The good news*: Church attendance rose dramatically the last three weeks.
  The bad news: You were on vacation.

Unfortunately, things aren't always as they first appear. The tables of life's events can turn quickly leaving you scratching your head. It can happen to overworked pastors, and as we will see in today's reading, it can happen to mighty kings.

Paul was still in custody in Caesarea when he was called to stand before the visiting monarch, his majesty, King Herod Agrippa. It was a big event and,

> *"...everybody who was anybody in Caesarea found his way to the Great Hall, along with the top military brass. Agrippa and Bernice made a flourishing grand entrance and took their places"*
> (Acts 25:23 *The Message*).

The Royalty had arrived. The purple was prominent and the jewels were dazzling. Trumpets blared and subjects bowed, all to pay homage to the visiting king. Yes, it looked like a good day for King Herod Agrippa. That is until the appearance of the prisoner Paul. His clothes were unkempt, his body unwashed, and his attitude unpretentious. "You may speak your defense," the opulent king announced, no doubt expecting a spectacular display of grovelling worthy of such a setting. But what his highness didn't know was that Paul was not there to ask the king for something, but rather to offer it. In verse six we see, Paul jumped right in.

> *"I am on trial because I hope for the promise that God made to our ancestors ... My king, they accuse me because I hope for this same promise!"*
> (Acts 26:6, 7b *The New Century Version*).

Paul turned the tables on the king. Instead of pleading for mercy from his wrath, Paul proclaimed hope in the amazing mercy of God. Hope in the fact that God always keeps His promises. Indeed by royal summons Paul was called to the gala, but not by King Agrippa. God had summoned him there to offer everyone present hope.

Good news; and then bad news. Maybe the gist of the Gospel message is that these are reversed. As singer/songwriter Steven Curtis Chapman put it, the *bad news* is, we're far worse off than we thought. And the *good news*? We're far more loved than we'd ever dreamed. And this is our hope.

The Original Missionary

READ ACTS 26:12-18

The mission field is vast. A lot can be said about the need for reaching out to foreign countries with the good news of God's love. At Crossroads, we have extensively assisted more than 70 countries to develop their own Christian television ministries. Many also make a difference personally by hand-delivering God's message of grace – an act of obedience in response to the call of God known as "The Great Commission." Jesus Himself commanded:

> *"Go into all the world and preach the Good News to everyone, everywhere"* (Mark 16:15).

For the last 2000 years millions have done just that. One such was a missionary to China.

Standard Oil had offered him an enormous sum of money to develop their Chinese venture. The missionary turned them down. They doubled the offer. He turned them down again. Dismayed they said, "What do you want? We can't give more money than that." He replied, "Money has nothing do to with it. When compared to my current position, your job is just too small."

This man took the Great Commission seriously. Apostle Paul did as well.

As a prisoner Paul was given an audience with King Herod Agrippa. It was an unprecedented opportunity for Paul to personally share the message of the Cross with one of the most renowned rulers of the land. Paul did so the same way many do today – by sharing his own personal encounter with Jesus:

"I used to believe that I ought to do everything I could to oppose the followers of Jesus ...One day... a light from heaven brighter than the sun shone down on me and my companions. We all fell down, and I heard a voice saying to me in Aramaic, 'Saul, Saul, why are you persecuting me?'...'Who are you, sir?' I asked. And the Lord replied, 'I am Jesus, the One you are persecuting'" (Acts 26:9, 13-15).

Even though he wasn't one of the original 12 disciples, Paul had a personal encounter with Jesus and it changed his life forever. From that moment, Paul was not only released from the bonds of hatred, he was freed from the cycle of sin – something we all need freedom from. That's why I'm so glad the story didn't end with Paul's enlightenment. Beginning in verse 17, let's find out what else Jesus said to Paul.

"I am going to send you to the Gentiles, to open their eyes so that they may turn from darkness to light, and from the power of Satan to God. Then they will receive forgiveness for their sins ..." (Acts 26:17b, 18).

Paul became a missionary to a huge group of people – the gentiles. Because a "gentile" is anyone who is not Jewish, in essence Paul was the original missionary to you and me. What an amazing thought! Paul's obedience in carrying out the Great Commission continues to influence us today.

What about our obedience? Once we've accepted God's Grace, shouldn't we all be missionaries? Our obedience to the Great Commission could have far greater impact than we could ever imagine. As one author put it, ultimately a missionary is only one beggar telling another beggar where to get food. He cannot give out of his bounty, for he has no bounty. He is simply a guest at his Master's table, calling others to come and eat too.

Almost Persuaded

READ ACTS 26:19-32

When I was growing up, saying good-bye was a way of life. My Dad was in the U.S. Army, and we moved every one to two years. Because everyone in the neighbourhood was enlisted in the army, all of my friends were in the same boat. "Good-bye" was a common phrase. I'll never forget my best friend Jackie. She had an especially difficult time saying good-bye. At that time we lived on an army base in North Carolina, and her father had just been transferred to Germany. For weeks the family prepared to go, saying good-bye to the close-knit group who knew all-too-well how hard it was to leave. But two days before they were to fly out, something devastating happened – devastating, that is, if you're 12 years old.

The family dog ran away. For the next 48 hours, everyone in the neighbourhood searched for "Bristles" without success. Finally, Jackie's family had to leave without their beloved dog. Before going, however, they left specific instructions that if he turned up, he was to be shipped to them in Germany. And that's when my home telephone rang.

Because I had spent so much time at Jackie's house, my phone number was the contact number for the pound. When they called to say that they had found a dog matching Bristle's description, my Dad immediately drove me there. I was so excited. I couldn't wait to see him. As we walked past the cages, I searched for his familiar face. The director stopped in front of me and pointed into a cage. "This is the one we phoned you about."

My heart sank. I looked into the mournful eyes of a tired brown dog. Bristles was gray. While the two dogs seemed to be close in appearance, they were worlds apart in identity. "Close" was not good enough to save Bristles. And neither was it good enough to save King Agrippa.

Paul continued to address the king, as well as the host of assembled dignitaries. He told of his amazing encounter with the risen Jesus on the road to Damascus and of Jesus' admonition to spread the good news of the Cross to everyone. His words moved the king. Paul said,

> *"...to this day I have had the help which comes from God [as my ally] ... asserting nothing beyond what the prophets and Moses declared would come to pass – That the Christ (the Anointed One) must suffer and that He, by being the first to rise from the dead, would declare and show light both to the [Jewish] people and to the Gentiles"* (Acts 26:22, 23 *The Amplified Bible*).

Several times Paul addressed his remarks specifically to the king. Although there was a great number in attendance, Paul seemed to be speaking to an audience of one. When he finished his message,

> *"Agrippa said unto Paul, 'Thou almost persuadest me to be a Christian'"* (Acts 26:28 *KJV*).

King Agrippa was *close* to being persuaded. But when it comes to getting right with God, we know "almost" will never do. Just like the identity of the dog, it's either genuine, or it's not. You've either been forgiven through the Blood of Jesus, or you have not. There is no middle ground. When committing your life to Jesus you commit your "all."

By the way, Bristles never turned up. Just like King Agrippa, he waited too late to come home.

Ship of Fools

READ ACTS 27:1-12

In 1965 there was a movie in theatres called, *Ship of Fools*. It's the story of a German ocean liner set in pre WWII days. While the movie presented this ship as a virtual microcosm of the pre-Nazi world, many reviewers painted it more as a floating soap opera. Even though it received eight Academy Award nominations, I haven't seen it. But something about it did grab my attention.

The author of the book on which the movie was based, Katherine Anne Porter, made a comment that caught my ear. When asked what prompted the concept of the story and more precisely, the title of the book, she said it represented the "simple almost universal image of the 'ship of this world' on its voyage to eternity." The ship of this world full of its achievers, loosers, and everyone in between. Basically, a ship of fools. Actually, that might be an apt description of the ship on which the apostle Paul sailed as a prisoner.

The ship of this world, full of its achievers, loosers, and everyone in between. Basically, a ship of fools.

The apostle Paul had been in prison for more than two years when he held his evangelistic audience with King Agrippa. His pardon was not granted and Paul was to be transported to Rome as a prisoner. This was a sequence of events that came as no surprise to him. In Acts 23, we read of one of his most terrifying moments in prison. Let's listen to a promise made to Paul by the Lord Himself.

> *"That night the Lord appeared to Paul and said, 'Be encouraged, Paul. Just as you have told the people about Me here in Jerusalem you must preach the Good News in Rome'"* (Acts 23:11).

And so Paul found himself on a ship bound for Rome – you could say his, "ship of fools." With the crew and guards on board this was a prison ship. It would be safe to assume that among the prisoners, Paul was the only Roman citizen, and therefore the only one with hope. More than likely, the prison ship carried criminals destined for execution. Many were likely to become gladiators, ultimately to be fed to wild animals. In those days a steady stream of people flowed into the Colosseum in Rome to provide gruesome entertainment for the masses. Paul's shipmates would have been without hope. What a gift these men were given in the hope-filled message of God's grace that Paul delivered! Further in the chapter we also read that he delivered a prophetic warning to those in charge of the ship:

> *"'Sirs,' he said, 'I believe there is trouble ahead if we go on – shipwreck, loss of cargo, injuries, and danger to our lives.' But the officer in charge of the prisoners listened more to the ship's captain and the owner than to Paul"* (Acts 27:10, 11).

Paul delivered a warning of storms ahead, but the officer in charge didn't listen. Trusting in himself, he was a fool among others on the way to their own destruction.

How like the "ship of this world on its voyage to eternity"! God sends us warnings of the storms ahead, but do we listen, or do we trust our own logic and discernment? Even if we miss it we can conquer the storms by keeping our "ship" anchored in the only Constant there is. The faithfulness of Almighty God.

Surviving Life's Storms

READ ACTS 27:13-26

It sometimes seems we just get through one storm when there's another one brewing on our horizon. Things wouldn't be so bad if hard times came with an attached summary of "the things you will learn as a result of this storm." At least then we'd be prepared for it.

Recently I came across a story of a little bird that illustrates how nice it would be to have good advice ahead of time when heading into a predicament. He was all alone flying south for the winter when he noticed the temperature drastically falling. Soon his beak was chattering from the cold and his wings were weighed down with icicles. The wind was so strong and he was so weak that finally he fell to the ground, completely frozen. There he lay, totally helpless in a large farm field. That's when he heard someone coming. "Oh good!" he thought. "Someone will help me, now." The "someone" turned out to be a cow, and instead of helping the bird, she deposited a pile of fresh manure on him. "Oh no!" he thought, "not this!" But as the little bird lay under the disgusting pile, he began to realize how warm it was. The manure was thawing him out! Warm and happy, he began singing for joy. A passing cat heard the little bird singing, and came to investigate. Discovering the bird under the pile of manure, the cat promptly dug him out and ate him!

The moral of the story is:

#1. Not everyone who drops manure on you is your enemy.

#2. Not everyone who digs you out of a pile of manure is your friend.

#3. When you're in the manure, keep your mouth shut!

#4. And finally, sometimes life stinks.

Some good advice for facing life's storms! And good advice in a storm is just what the apostle Paul was giving in our reading for today.

Paul was a prisoner on a prison ship ultimatly destined for Rome. Several times the weather had hampered their progress, pushing them out to sea to helplessly ride out the strong winds. However, to this latest storm there was no end. In fact, the crew began to panic, and to "throw out the ship's equipment and anything else they could lay their hands on." (*Acts 27:18-19*) We read,

> *"The terrible storm raged unabated for many days, blotting out the sun and the stars, until at last all hope was gone"* (Acts 27:20).

As is often the case, when all hope fades, we realize how "almighty" God is. And in verse 22, that's exactly the message God delivered through the apostle Paul. He said to the men on board,

> *"... take courage!... For last night an angel of the God to whom I belong and whom I serve stood beside me, and he said, 'Don't be afraid, Paul ... God in His goodness has granted safety to everyone sailing with you.' So take courage! For I believe God"* (Acts 27:23-25a).

Do you need good advice? Do you need courage? Do you need someone to believe in? Is your storm tearing your world apart leaving you desperate and without hope?

Believe in Jesus. He understands and he can carry you through. He loves you so much that He chose to become a man and go through every storm you will ever face. Walk with Him through life's storms and take His advice. You need never be alone again.

Be Still and Know That He is God

READ ACTS 27:27-44

I flicked on the interior light of the car just long enough to have a glimpse at the map. "If it were daylight," I said to my husband, "we'd be overlooking the beautiful Appalachian Mountains." My parents lived in North Carolina, and to visit them, we often drove through the night. Besides saving time and the cost of a hotel room, Ron and I enjoyed the quiet of the car while the kids slept in their seats. You can cover a lot of ground in the middle of the night when the roads are mostly empty and you have nothing but time. Just like on this night, we spent most of that time talking about anything and everything just to stay awake.

It was around 3:00 a.m. – that pitch-black time of night when you're still far enough from morning that it feels the night will never end. The highway had climbed steadily up a mountain where there are no street lights, no farm houses, and no lights of any kind other than the headlights of your own car. And that's when we noticed it. The inky night around us was enveloping us with a thick layer of fog. Within seconds, the fog was so thick that we could not see beyond the end of our car. We could do nothing but stop. We knew that on one side of us was the mountain face going straight up, and on the other, was the cliff going straight down. The fog was so thick that we couldn't see either. And so there we sat, in the middle of highway, in the middle of the night, frozen with fear and completely helpless. Well, almost. Ron and I began to pray. Before long we noticed the headlights of a large truck coming up behind us. We were never so happy to see anyone. He flashed his brights, passed us slowly, and inched along in front of us, using his four-way flashers to lead us down the mountain.

That night, high on that deserted mountain road, God sent us direction in the form of an 18-wheeler. Maybe a bit unusual, but no more so than the deliverance he sent the apostle Paul.

Paul was a prisoner on a ship bound for Rome when a great storm arose – and continued – for two weeks. Hope only came as they finally spotted an unfamiliar shore. However, there they became stuck on a sandbank where the waves constantly battered the hull. The crew's thought was to abandon ship, but they were concerned what the prisoners might do. Once on the island, who knew what would happen?

> *"The soldiers wanted to kill the prisoners to make sure they didn't swim ashore and escape. But the commanding officer wanted to spare Paul, so he didn't let them carry out their plan"* (Acts 27:42, 43a).

Even while the ship was sinking, God had a plan. Through an angel, He had already told Paul that no one on the ship would die. And if He had to use the commanding officer of Paul's captors to fulfill His plan, that's just what He would do.

How about you? Do you ever feel shipwrecked because of storms in your life or deserted in a mountain of fog? Are you searching for "God's Plan" for your life? Stand still. Be quiet. Know that He is God. And know that as you trust in Him, He will keep you moving forward according to His plan.

Stand still.
Be quiet.
Know that He is God.

Jumping to Conclusions?

READ ACTS 28:1-16

From time to time we're all guilty of jumping to conclusions. Most of the time, the consequences of our mental leap-frog are minimal. But recently I came across an article from a July 1993 edition of *The San Francisco Examiner* that illustrated how sometimes "conclusion jumping" can be costly.

The California Automobile Association claims office had just received a package by Federal Express. The unknown contents were securely enclosed in a Fruit Loops cereal box, which immediately aroused suspicion. Even back then the authorities were alert for terrorist bombings, and as a result all 400 office workers were evacuated. The bomb squad was called and when it arrived it promptly neutralized the Fruit Loops box with a small cannon, blasting its contents into the air. As the authorities got their first up-close look, they found no explosives. Rather, inside the suspicious package were bundles of $20 bills – adding up to $24,000. The blast of the cannon destroyed more than $1,000.

"We always try to err on the side of caution," the supervising officer said. Of course, that's a good thing where safety is concerned. However, as we'll see in today's reading, an error in judgement took place when certain island natives did a little "conclusion jumping" of their own.

The apostle Paul and his 275 shipmates had abandoned ship and made it safely to the island of Malta. It was rainy and cold and the people of the island were very kind to the shipwrecked men. They promptly built a large fire for Paul and his companions. However, trouble struck:

> *"[Paul] had gathered up a bundle of sticks, but when he put it on the fire, a venomous snake, roused from its [idleness] by the heat, struck his hand an held on. Seeing the snake hanging from Paul's hand like that, the natives jumped to the conclusion that he was a murderer getting his just deserts"* (Acts 28:3, 4 *The Message*).

Evidently these natives believed in justice. One Bible scholar said these people thought there was a god named "justice" who would punish bad people. When the snake attacked Paul, they *knew* he was getting what he deserved, and they waited for the inevitable:

> *"The people thought that Paul would swell up or fall down dead. They waited and watched him for a long time, but nothing bad happened to him. So they changed their minds and said, 'He is a god!'"* (Acts 28:6 *The New Century Version*).

Once again, the people jumped to conclusions. Paul was not a murderer, and he was not a god. He was merely a man walking in complete obedience to God, under His almighty protection.

In our world, we're quick to jump to conclusions. We want justice at any cost. And while justice is God's stand against sin, let's not forget His provision for sinful man – the "conclusion" that's available for us all. Through the Cross of Jesus, God graciously fulfilled the requirements of justice – by hand-delivering mercy.

Through the Cross of Jesus, God graciously fulfilled the requirements of justice – by hand-delivering mercy.

A Fool for Christ

READ ACTS 28:17-31

After spending three months shipwrecked on an island, the apostle Paul arrived under armed guard in the city of Rome. The Lord Himself had told Paul in a dream that he would indeed go there to preach the message of the Cross.

Once in Rome Paul was treated well. He was permitted to have his own private lodging, though he was guarded by a soldier. And only three days after his arrival, he called together the city's Jewish leaders. This was an extension of the same group of men who had several times plotted to kill him, and eventually had him imprisoned. Shouldn't Paul have been a little wary to call these men together? He was definitely in the minority. But as we'll see, there wasn't the same hatred in Rome against Paul as there was in Jerusalem. In fact, they told him,

> *"We have heard nothing against you ... we want to hear what you believe"* (Acts 28:21a, 22a).

These Jewish leaders had no reason to condemn Paul. He was in a new city. All he had to do was to keep quiet about his stand for Jesus and they would have had no claim against him. But Paul couldn't do that. He had discovered the truth of God's grace through the Cross and he could not keep it to himself. And so, without reservation, Paul shared the love of God. Sounds a lot like another young man, right off the pages of our newspapers.

In May 2000, the *Columbus Dispatch* that serves Columbus Ohio, reported an amazing story of a young man's bold stand for Christ at Upper Arlington High School. Justin Rule first gained attention with his outspoken belief in Jesus. While his reputation as a "Jesus freak" spread throughout the school of 1,800 kids, Justin won kids to Christ. In the "politically correct" atmosphere of today's public high schools, it isn't acceptable to express one's faith blatantly. But God always provides a way. Teenage ingenuity kicked in. Bright yellow t-shirts began showing up in Upper Arlington High School. Shirts that all carried the same simple message: "I agree with Justin." And soon hundreds of kids were wearing them. When the *Columbus Dispatch* interviewed Justin about this phenomenon, he simply said, "It's not about religion. It's not about a group. It's about the truth that I found. And I can't keep it inside."

Taking a stand for Christ. Is it scary? Yes. Is it worth it? Definitely. Noted speaker William Carey once made the statement, "Expect great things from God. Attempt great things for God." Justin did. Paul did. And so can you!

> *"Expect great things from God. Attempt great things for God."*
> *~ William Carey*

The Crossroads Ministry Story

It All Began In 1962...

In Pembroke, located in the Ottawa Valley of north-eastern Ontario, David Mainse was the pastor of an area church. It was there, in 1962, David and his wife Norma-Jean first broadcast the Gospel on black and white TV sets. The program was called *Crossroads.*

As the Mainse family moved to other centres to pastor, the television ministry moved with them. It grew in popularity and was aired on more and more stations.

In 1977, the ministry of Crossroads launched daily programming across Canada from God-given facilities in downtown Toronto at an address after which the telecast was named: ***100 Huntley Street.***

Crossroads' Mission Statement

"The key objective of Crossroads Christian Communications Incorporated is to add to and bring unity to the body of Christ through direct and indirect evangelism; to enhance and augment the ministry of the local church; and to build understanding, credibility and attractiveness of life in Jesus Christ.

"This will be accomplished by the creative use of television and other media, together with other activities which respond to the mission conscience and needs of the constituency. The responsibility for outreach is to the world. Outside North America, C.C.C.I. responds only to the requests from organized and established Christian leadership. The role is as a catalyst to the development of indigenous and self-supporting ministry."

Accountability

Crossroads Christian Communications Inc. is federally chartered in both Canada and the United States as a charitable, non-profit organization. As such, it is funded wholly through free-will offerings. Crossroads is audited annually by Price Waterhouse Lybrand. Financial statements are available upon written request.

Crossroads receives the annual Seal of Financial Accountability from the Canadian Council of Christian Charities.

Ron & Ann

Rhonda

Norm

David & Norma-Jean

Reynold & Kathy

The Crossroads Family of Ministries is made possible through the generous gifts of people like you who believe in Life-Changing Television. As many as 1.5 million individuals tune in to the *100 Huntley Street* broadcast every week.

24-Hour Prayer Ministry

Prayer lines are available 24 hours a day – a lifeline for many in crisis.

Crossroads receives calls from over 30,000 needy people each month. Over 200 volunteer prayer partners donate 30,000 hours each year to minister and pray for such needs as salvation, healing, substance abuse, suicide, emotional problems and family concerns.

Crossroads also provides helpful ministry materials on many relevant subjects like anger, depression, grief, healing, reconciliation, etc.

To help new Christians become firmly established in their relationship with God, Crossroads uses in-depth Bible study courses. New Christians are also encouraged to join a local church for further spiritual growth and fellowship with other believers.
A Crossroads prayer partner would love to pray with you for any special need you may be facing today. Simply call our prayer line nearest you.

Crossroads Prayer Lines

A Crossroads prayer partner would love to pray with you for any special need you may be facing today. Simply call our prayer line nearest you:

Vancouver, BC	**604-430-1212**
Calgary, AB	**403-284-4721**
Edmonton, AB	**780-944-0742**
Regina, SK	**306-781-8970**
Winnipeg, MB	**204-949-9414**
London, ON	**519-488-1638**
Burlington, ON or USA	**905-335-0100**
Toronto, ON	**416-929-1500**
Ottawa, ON	**613-482-2264**
Montreal, QC	**514-935-8814**
Quebec City, QC	**418-864-7448**
Saint John, NB	**506-674-2400**
Halifax, NS	**902-455-2600**
St. John's, NF	**709-738-2731**
Hearing impaired TDD	**905-335-6104**

A Special Invitation: If you live in the Toronto/Burlington area and would like to join the ministry as a prayer partner, call the National Ministry Centre at:

905-332-6400, ext. 2383

The Crossroads Conway School of Broadcasting

The television production and course at the Crossroads Conway School of Broadcasting is a comprehensive training program. It is designed to prepare those with a vision to start Christian programming in their own countries and combines classroom study with hands-on practical experience. Crossroads has trained over 1,350 students from 70 countries and there are now over 40 Christian television ministries which have begun as a direct result of our graduates.

Circle
Square
Ranch
HOTEL
CIRCLE SQUARE
FIRST
NATIONAL BANK
BAKERY
TELEGRAPH
OFFICE
WELLS FARGO

Crossroads Missions

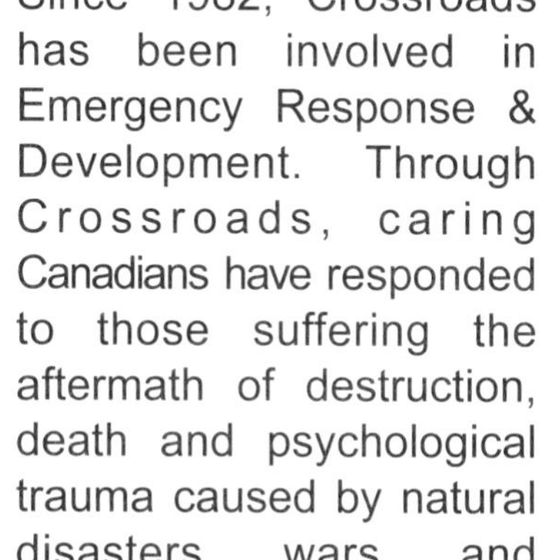
Since 1982, Crossroads has been involved in Emergency Response & Development. Through Crossroads, caring Canadians have responded to those suffering the aftermath of destruction, death and psychological trauma caused by natural disasters, wars, and extreme poverty in the developing world.

The Walk of Faith

The Walk of Faith is a lovely walkway near the entrance of the Crossroads Centre. Along the walkway are engraved granite stones which have been donated in honour or in memory of special people. At the top of this area stands the "Freedom Flagpole" dedicated to God as a monument to the acheivement of Crossroads becoming debt free in 2004. At the very top flies the Canadian flag saluting our national unity and God's dominion from sea to sea. To find out how you can honour someone on the Walk of Faith call:

1-800-265-3100

Other Crossroads Outreaches Sharing The Love of Jesus...

Nite Lite
Middle-of-the-night open-line ministry.

T.Q.
Saturday morning children's programming with a positive message.

Huntley Street Radio
□life-changing radio□ with Ron and Ann Mainse in a weekday broadcast featuring outstanding guests from the international television program, *100 Huntley Street.*

CARD TRICKS

TOP THAT! Kids™

Top That! USA, 27023 McBean Parkway, #408 Valencia, CA 91355

www.topthatpublishing.com

Perfect Patter

This is really important! If you draw your audience into your performance with some really slick chat, you will divert their attention from what you are doing with your hands!

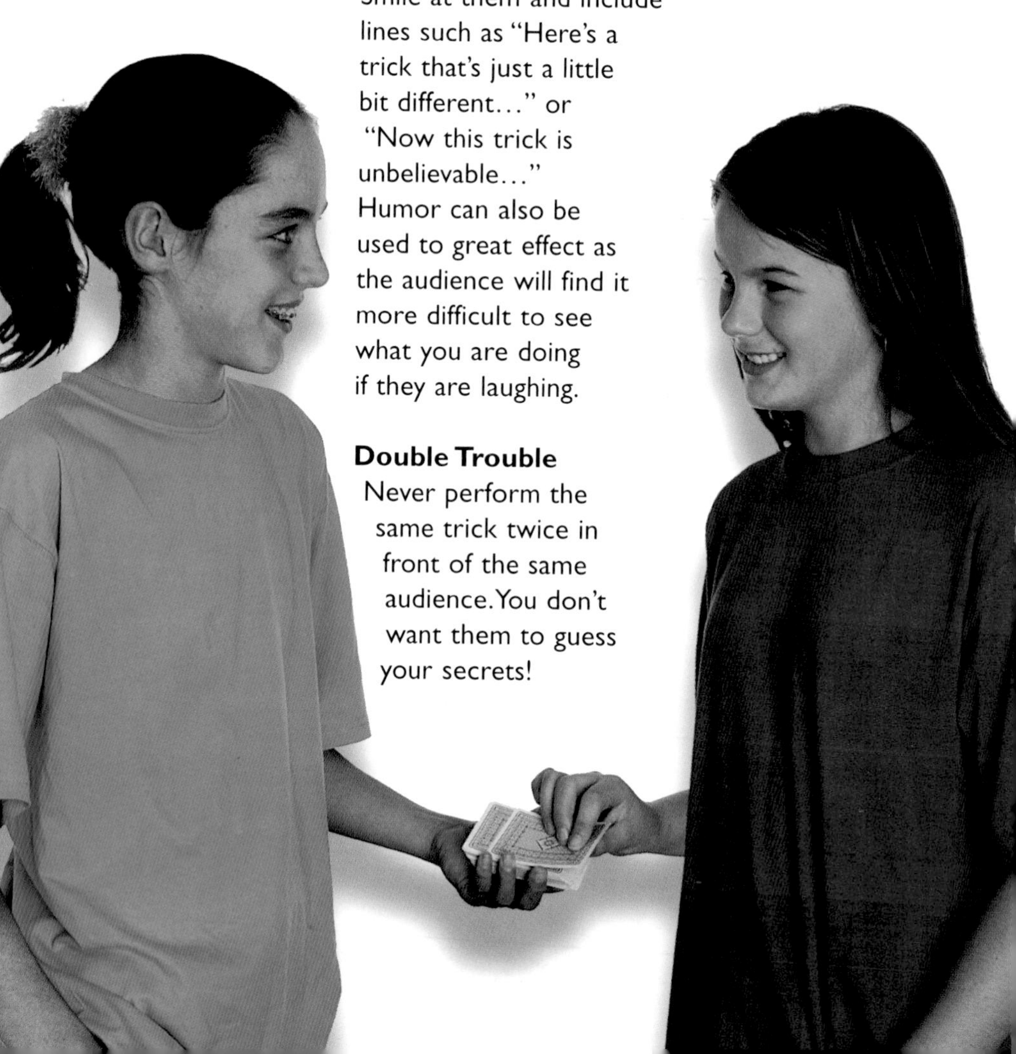

Smile!

Smile at them and include lines such as "Here's a trick that's just a little bit different..." or "Now this trick is unbelievable..." Humor can also be used to great effect as the audience will find it more difficult to see what you are doing if they are laughing.

Double Trouble

Never perform the same trick twice in front of the same audience. You don't want them to guess your secrets!

Practice, Practice, Practice

The importance of practice should never be underestimated!

Make it Easy

The more you practice the more you will be able to make the most complicated tricks look effortless, and it will really boost your confidence for when it's time to perform. As you start to improve you'll be able to attempt more difficult illusions, and can even start creating your own!

Be Confident

Practice is also important when it comes to shuffling the cards. It may take a little while to feel completely confident holding a deck of cards and shuffling them between your hands. Make sure you can do this with ease before you perform any of the tricks.

Cutting the Cards and Shaping the Fan

Before you can become a real card magician you need to learn a few basics. Here's a good place to start.

1. Lift off around half the deck and place it to one side.

2. Take what was the bottom half and put it on top of the other pile. You have now cut the cards.

3. Now it's time to make the deck into a fan shape. Hold the deck in your left hand, making sure your thumb touches the lower end of the deck.

4. Put your right hand on the deck with your fingers at one end and your thumb at the other. Bend the cards over your left forefinger. Move your right hand in a circular motion to the right, letting the cards fan out from your fingers.

5. When all the cards are spread, you have completed the fan shape.

Sneaky Cut

Make it look as if you have cut the cards when really you haven't changed the order at all!

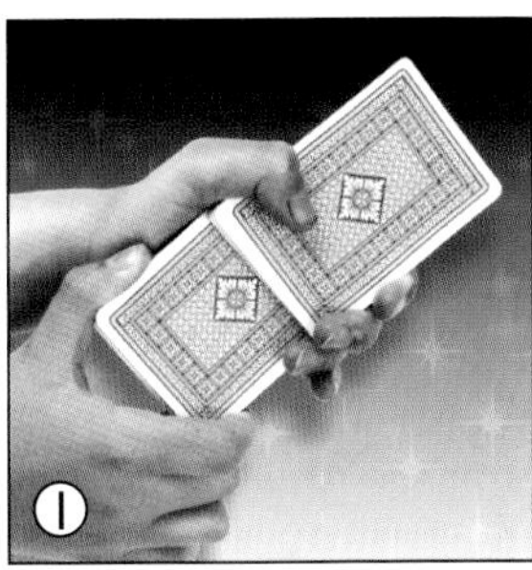

1. Hold the deck in your left hand and take about half the cards off from the bottom with your right hand.

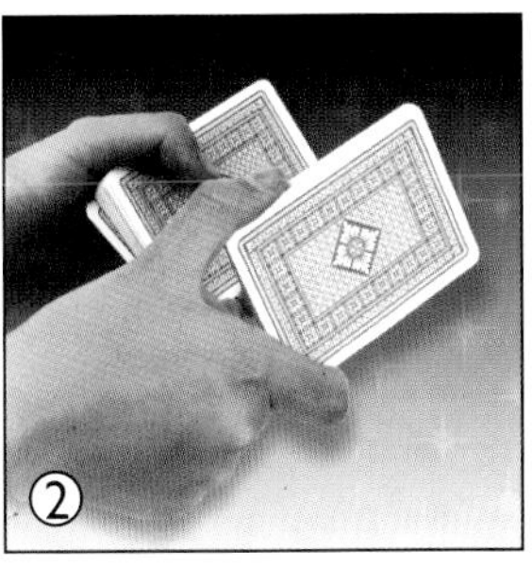

2. Bring the bottom cards towards your body. Now take them over the cards in your left hand and place them down on the table.

3. Take the top half of the deck in your right hand, moving your right hand slightly upwards.

4. Place the cards on top of the ones on the table.

④

Pick a Card

Force someone to choose the card you want them to without them realizing!

1. Shuffle the deck, but while you are shuffling, angle the cards so you can sneak a peak at the bottom card. Complete the shuffle, making sure you remember the bottom card.

2. Hold the deck behind your back and turn around so you are facing away from your audience. Ask a volunteer to take some cards from the top of the deck. When this is done turn around. As you do this, secretly move the card you remembered from the bottom of the deck to the top.

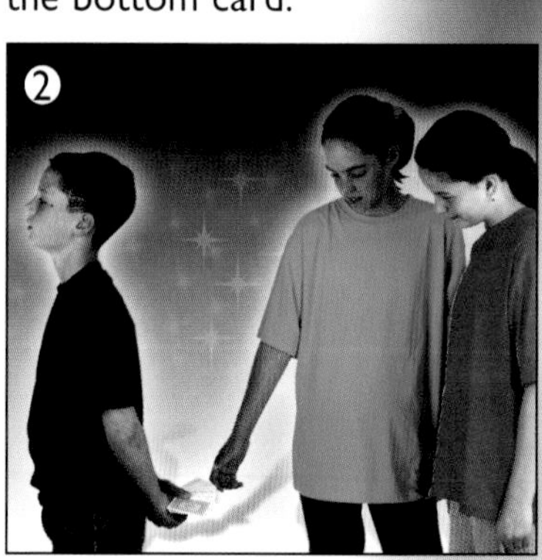

3. Tell your volunteer that enough cards have been taken. Then say, "Will you take the next card please?"

4. Then, ask them to hand the card back to you. Taking care not to look at it, hold the card up to your volunteer so that they can see the face.

5. If the card you remembered was, for example, the ace of hearts, ask your volunteer if that is their card. They will be amazed that you are right!

④

Overhand Shuffle

All card players use this simple shuffling technique.

1. Hold the cards in your left hand, as in the picture.

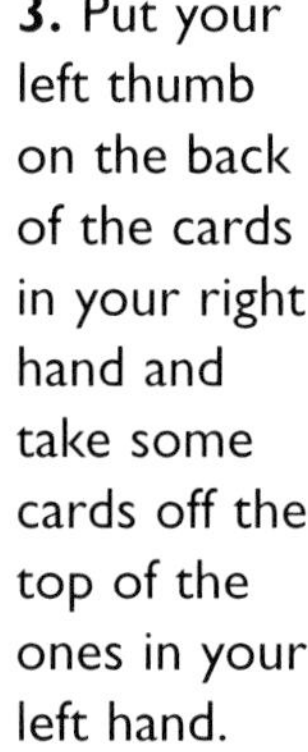

3. Put your left thumb on the back of the cards in your right hand and take some cards off the top of the ones in your left hand.

2. Take most of the bottom half of the cards with your right hand and lift them over the cards in your left hand.

4. Keep repeating this action until all the cards are in your left hand.

Shuffle Management

Your chosen card will be on top of the deck, even after shuffling!

1. Shuffle the cards and spread them out into a fan. Ask a volunteer to take a card and remember it. Now ask them to put it back, this time on top of the deck.

2. When the chosen card is put back on the deck, give the deck an overhand shuffle (see page 10). When you shuffle make sure you don't lose track of the chosen card. Do this by simply making sure it goes from the top of the deck to the bottom.

3. Do another overhand shuffle, but this time keep going until you have only the chosen card in your right hand. Then simply drop it back on top of the deck.

Feel the Force

This is another way of forcing someone to take the card of your choice.

1. The card that you will force someone to choose is at the bottom of the deck, so before you begin the trick, take a secret look at that card and remember it.

2. Tell a volunteer from your audience that you will force them to choose a card and name the card from the bottom of the deck. Hold the cards in your left hand, and place your right hand on top of them, with your right thumb underneath.

3. With the fingers of your right hand, move the cards back a few at a time. Ask your volunteer to say "stop" at any time while you are doing this.

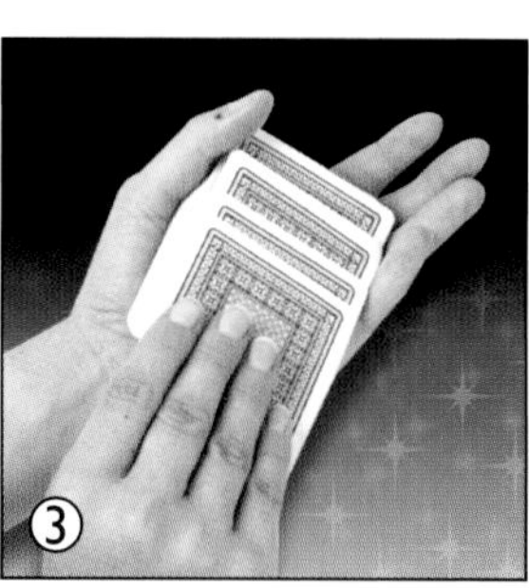

4. Pull back all the cards you have moved with your right hand. At the same time, drag the bottom card with your right thumb so that it is underneath the cards in your right hand. Hold up these cards to show the bottom one—it is, of course, the card which you told your audience you would find in step 2.

Spread

You will often need to display all the cards. One way is to spread the cards out evenly on a table.

1. Lay the deck on the table.

2. Lay your right hand flat on top of the deck, making sure your fingers extend beyond the edge of the cards.

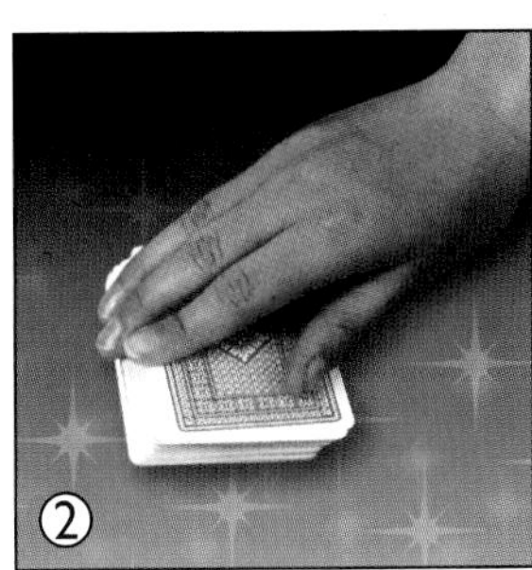

3. Push down lightly and move your hand to the right. The cards will spread out from the bottom, moved by your fingertips.

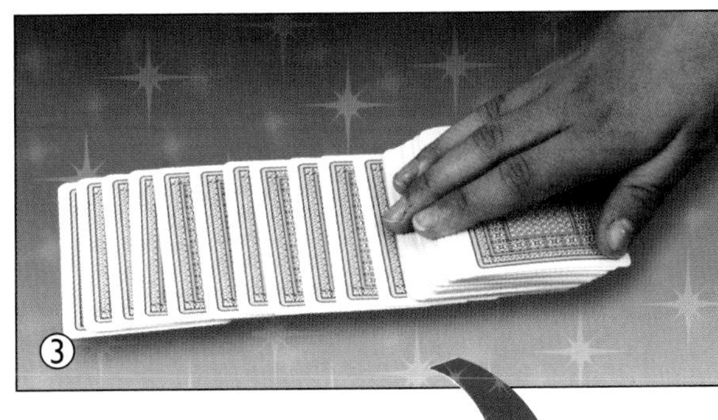

Pro Tip

This may take some practice but when you get it right, your routine will seem really sharp!

One Good Turn

You'll look very cool with this neat move!

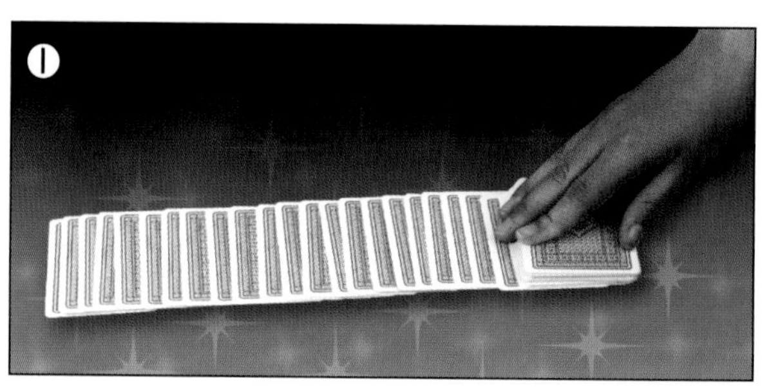

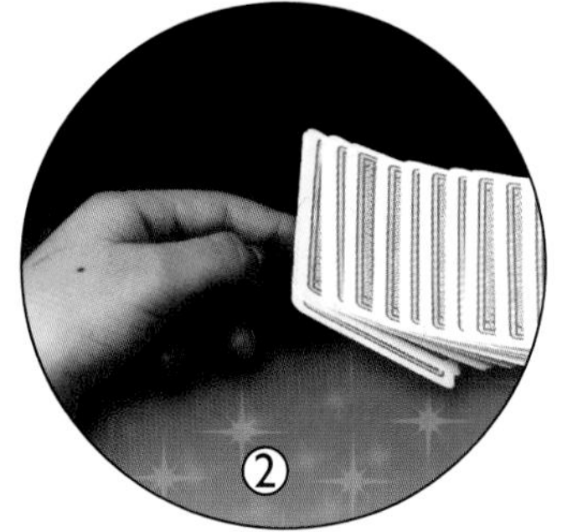

1. Lay the cards face down on a flat surface. Make sure you spread them out evenly. If they are not even, the trick will not work very well.

2. Put your left forefinger under the card furthest to the left.

3. Lift the side of the card up and then push it over so it is face up. This will make all the other cards turn over as well.

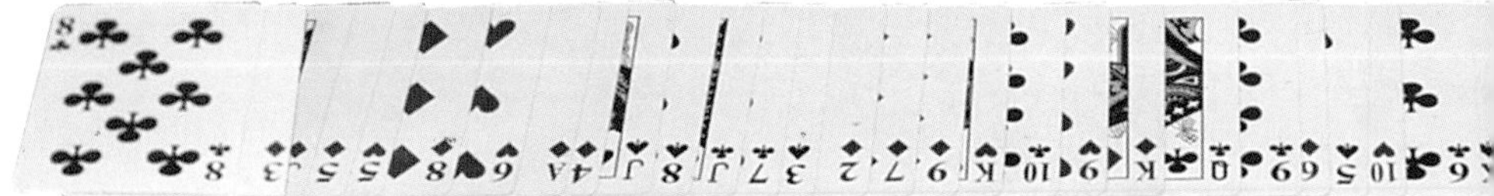

Pro Tip

Practice your tricks on your own first, then you will really impress your audience when you perform them for real!

Top Deck

Convince your audience that you have X-ray vision!

①

1. Before doing this trick, carefully cut a small window in the card box, so you can see the index corner of the top card.

③

2. Shuffle the deck of cards and return it to its box.

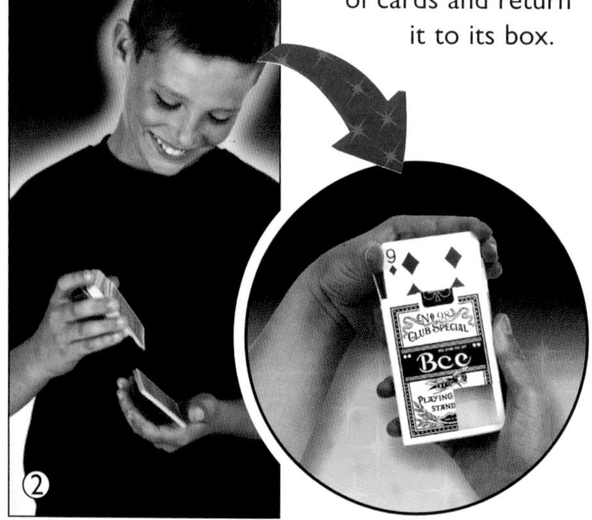

②

3. Name a card, then remove the deck from the box. The card you named is on the bottom!

4. Amazingly, you are right! Reshuffle the deck and repeat the trick.

Vanishing Ace

Make an ace disappear—and then appear somewhere else, as if by magic!

1. Secretly hide the ace of diamonds, somewhere in the room.

②

2. Show the other three aces to your audience, holding them so only the tip of the ace of hearts is showing. Point out to your audience that you are holding the ace of clubs, the ace of diamonds and the ace of spades, and that you are going to make the ace of diamonds disappear.

3. Turn the cards over and return them to the deck in different places.

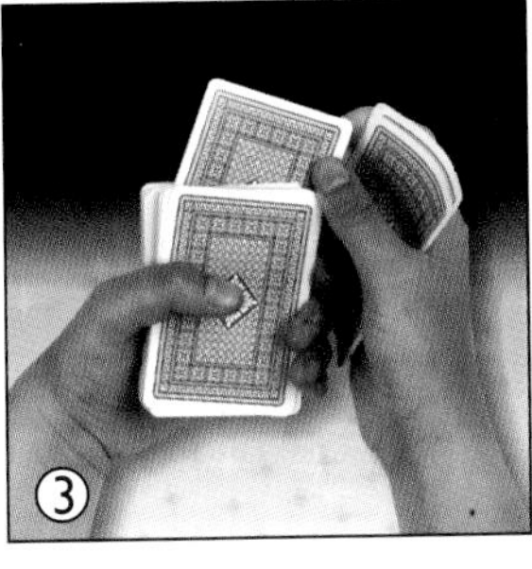

③

Shuffle the cards yourself, or pass them to a volunteer to shuffle.

4. Invite a volunteer to take out the ace of diamonds. It's not there!

④

5. Now ask someone else to go to the hiding place. Surprise! There is the missing ace.

⑤

King for a Day

You'll need a white candle and some white envelopes for this trick!

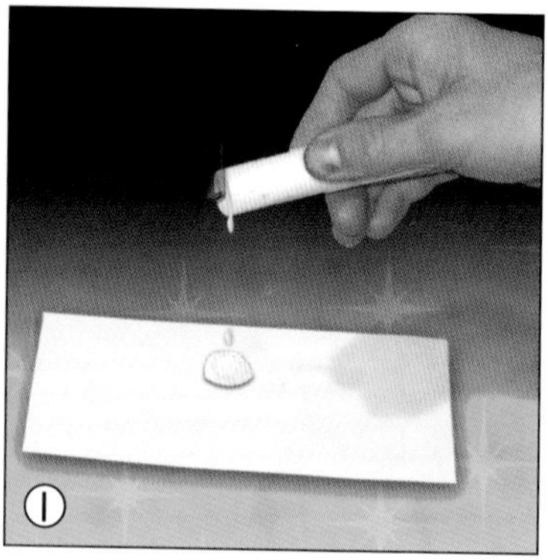

①

②

1. Before you start, ask an adult to light a white candle and drip a little bit of wax on one of the envelopes.

2. Put four jacks, four queens and a king into nine different envelopes. It doesn't matter which envelopes you put the jacks and queens in, but make sure the king goes in the envelope with the wax on it.

3. Ask a volunteer to mix up the envelopes and hand them to you one at a time. By touching the envelopes you will be able to tell when you receive the envelope containing the king.

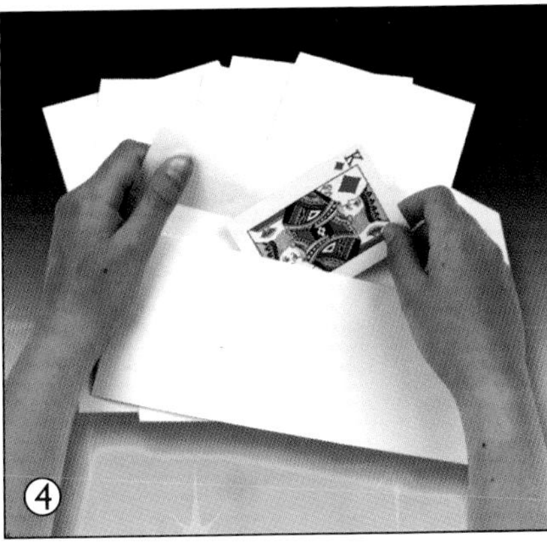

4. Open the envelope, saying you believe it is the one containing the king. Everyone will be amazed by your uncanny abilities.

Lucky Sixes

Take out all the sixes from the deck—behind your back!

①

1. Before you start this trick, take out the sixes and tuck them into your waistband or belt. Later, you will lift them out while you have your hands behind you.

2. Hand out the deck of cards for someone to shuffle for you.

3. Ask for the deck back and hold it behind your back. Announce that you will now remove all four sixes—which you do, with a flourish.

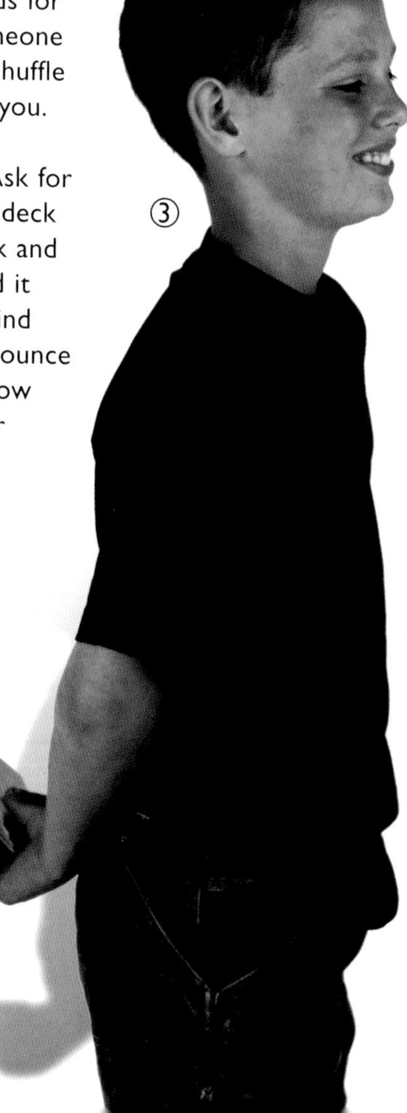
③

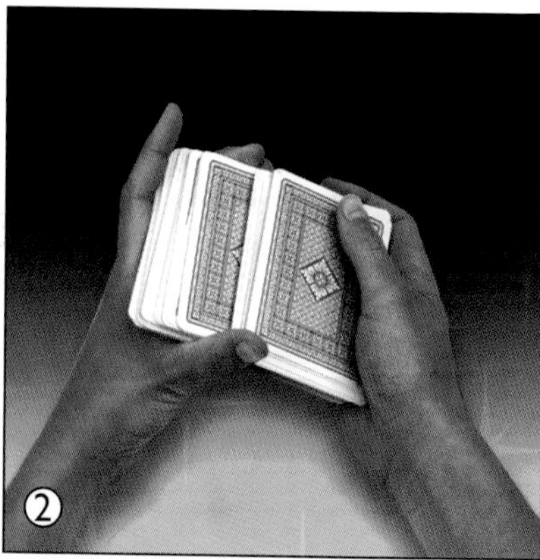
②

Royal Bag

Find the four kings inside a paper bag!

1. Show the audience an empty paper bag, then remove the four kings from the deck.

2. Fan out the four cards for the audience, secretly clipping them together at the bottom corner with a paper clip. Practice fixing and removing the paper clip smoothly.

3. Swiftly put the cards back into the deck and drop it into the paper bag. Give the bag a good shake.

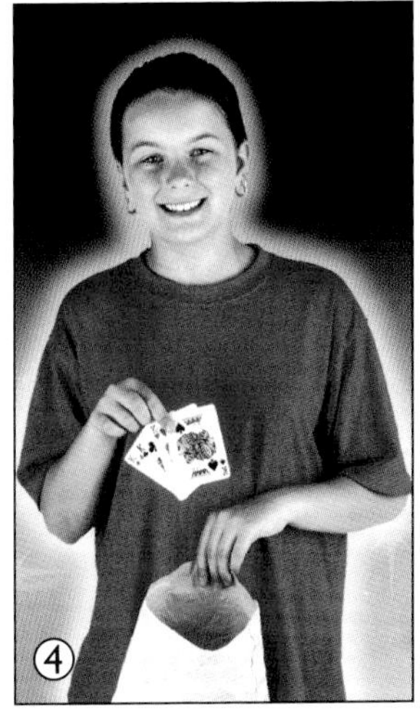

4. With a serious "flexing" of magic fingers, declare that you are going to retrieve the four kings. Put your hand into the bag, feel for the paper clip, and pull out the four cards, ensuring that the paper clip drops back into the bag.

Bottoms Up!

Before you perform this trick, make sure you turn the bottom card of the deck face up.

1. Spread the cards face down and then ask a volunteer to pick a card. When you are doing this, you must conceal the fact that the bottom card is turned up.

2. Ask your volunteer to display the card to the rest of the audience. As you are saying this, transfer the deck from one hand to the other, turning it over at the same time.

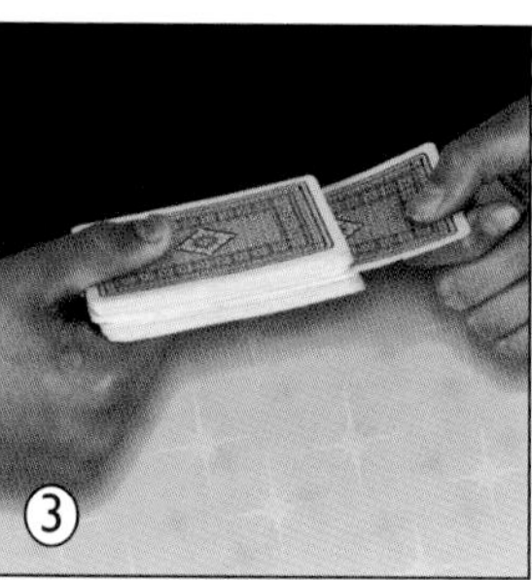

3. Ask your volunteer to push their chosen card face down into the deck. Hold the deck firmly as this is done as you don't want your volunteer to notice that the cards are really face up.

4. Take the cards behind your back, remove the reversed card, turn it over, and return it to the deck.

5. Put the deck on the table. Turn the cards over one by one and put them to one side. Use your patter, saying things like "I'm getting a strong feeling about your card." When you get to the chosen card it will of course already be face up. Now's the time to ask, "Is this your card?"

Surprise Fours

Find a chosen card—and four surprises!

1. Before you start, turn over a five and put it on top of the deck. On top of that, put all the fours, face down.

2. Ask a member of your audience to choose a card. Put it on the bottom of the deck.

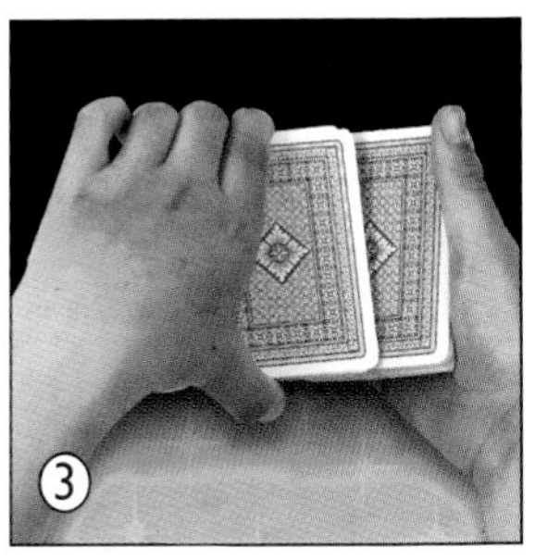

3. Cut the deck, so the chosen card is now next to the top of the fours.

4. Spread out the cards until you come to the reversed five.

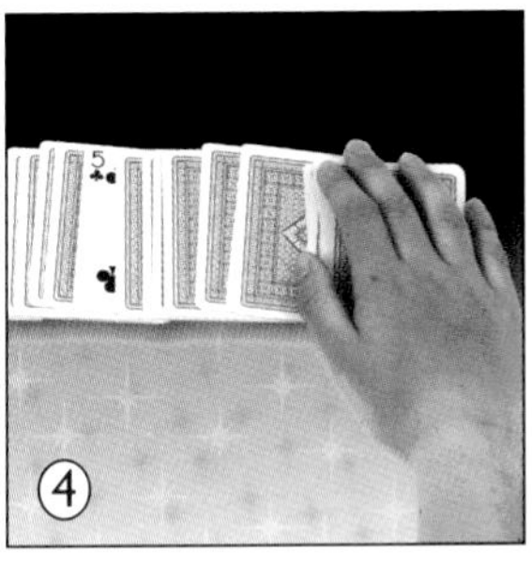

5. Count five cards along and push out the chosen card. Take away all the cards to the right of the chosen card and to the left of the five, so you are left with six cards on the table.

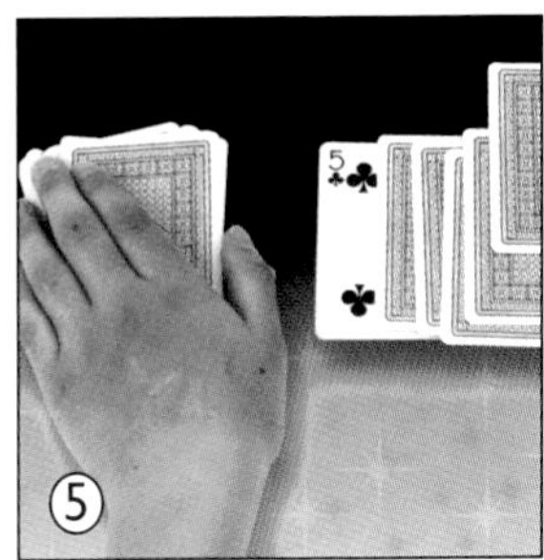

6. Reveal the chosen card for the audience to see, and stop as if the trick is finished. Then say "But here is something more amazing"—and turn up all the fours!

Magic Fingers

Nimble fingers magically sort the cards!

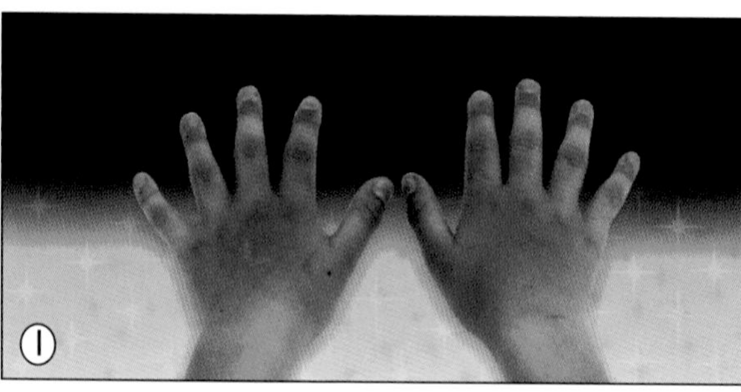

1. Ask someone to hold out their hands with their fingers touching the table top, just as if they were playing the piano.

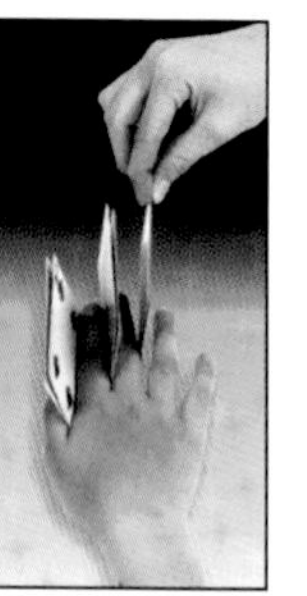

2. Take pairs of cards from a deck and place them between the fingers of each hand, calling out "Even" each time.

3. Do this with all the spaces between the fingers, except one. Into this last space put one card and say "Odd." The rest of the cards may be put aside.

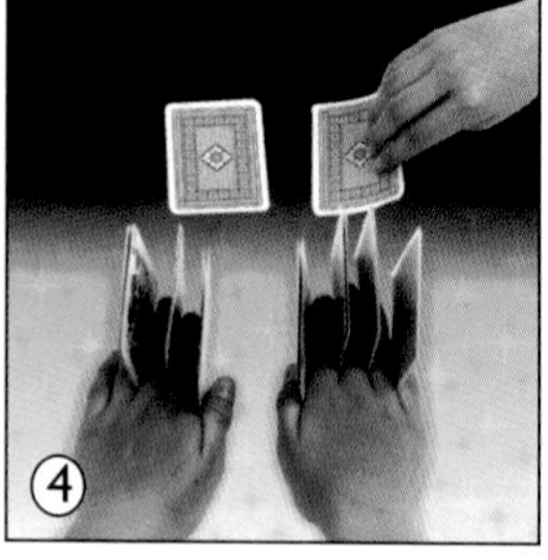

4. Take each pair of cards from between the fingers and lay them side by side face down on the table, to make two piles, saying "Even" each time.

5. Now take the single card. Let your volunteer choose which pile to place it on. Tap both piles and say you will now make the "odd" card jump from one pile to the other.

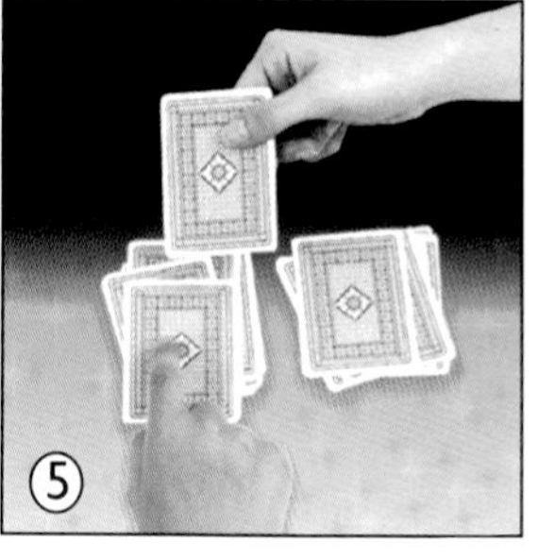

6. Deal out cards from the chosen pile in pairs, saying "Even" each time. Amazingly, it will now be even.

7. Do the same with the other pile, dealing out pairs, and you will be left with one "odd" card, just as you promised!

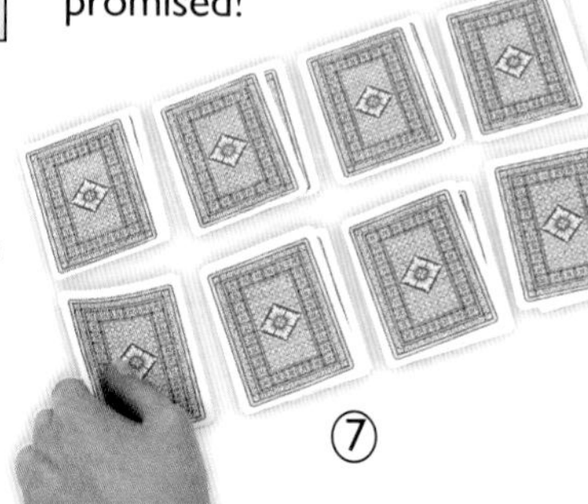

Telepathy Test

Demonstrate your baffling powers!

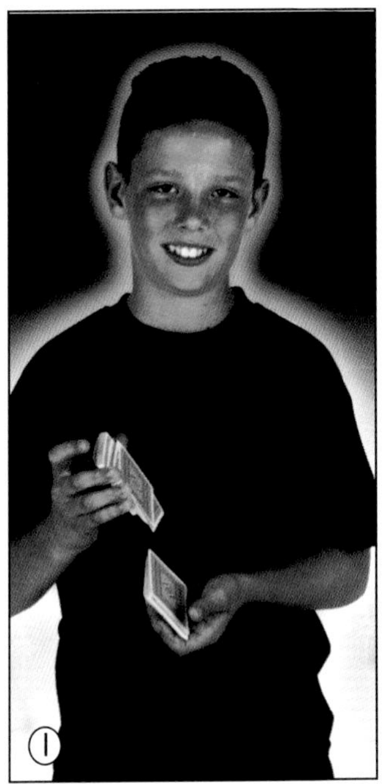

1. Shuffle a deck of cards and lay nine cards face up on the table in three rows of three.

2. Give the rest of the deck to a "volunteer." Explain you will leave the room for a few moments so the audience can choose one of the cards on the table.

3. Return to the room. Make a play of concentrating, then announce the number chosen.

How?

Your volunteer must be your secret assistant. Imagine the deck of cards divided into a grid, matching the one on the table. The assistant just needs to hold the deck with their thumb on the imaginary square indicating the card chosen.

Runaway Couple

Find a pair of cards hidden in the deck!

①

3. Hold the deck between finger and thumb. Give a quick flip so that the cards fly out of your hand, but keep hold of the top and bottom cards.

1. Before doing this trick, put the eight of diamonds on the bottom of the deck and the seven of hearts on the top. Return the deck to its box.

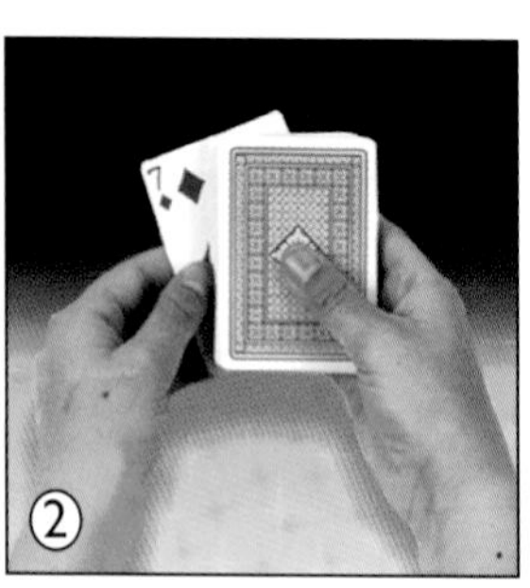
②

2. Hold up the deck, look through it and take out the seven of diamonds and eight of hearts. Hold them up quickly to your audience and say, "I am now going to put these into the center of the deck... and then I shall use my amazing powers to find them again."

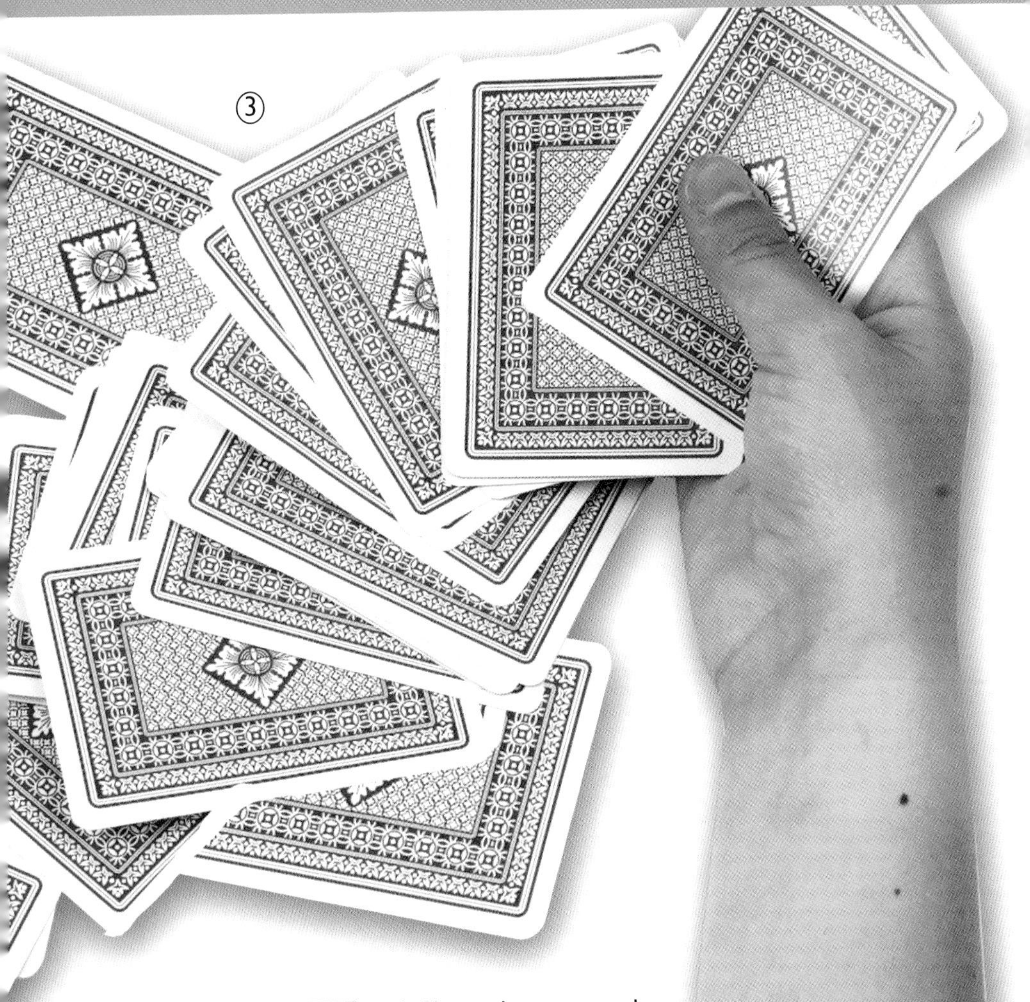

③

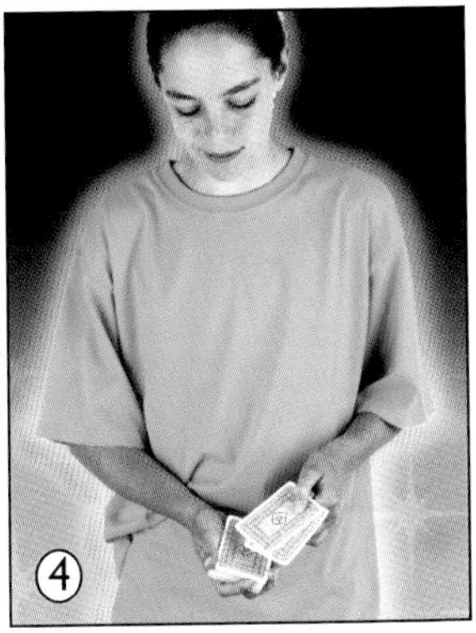

④

4. Show the two cards left in your hand and take a bow. As long as you did not draw attention to the face values, the audience will not notice that the cards have changed.

Going by Tube

You will need a length of cord or string and an empty card box (or any handy tube will do) for this great trick!

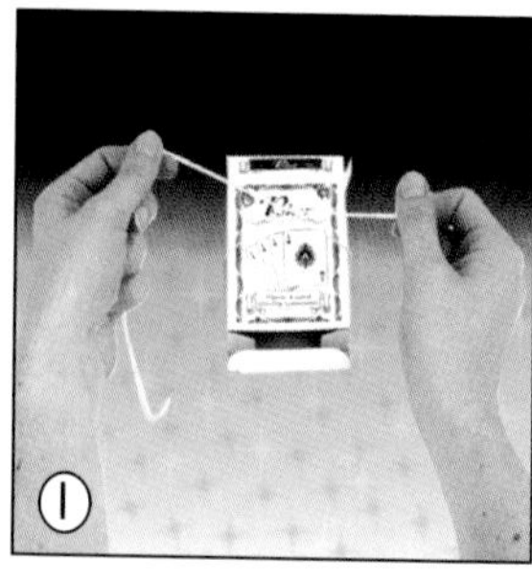

1. Loop the string around the outside of the box or tube. Tie a simple overhand knot.

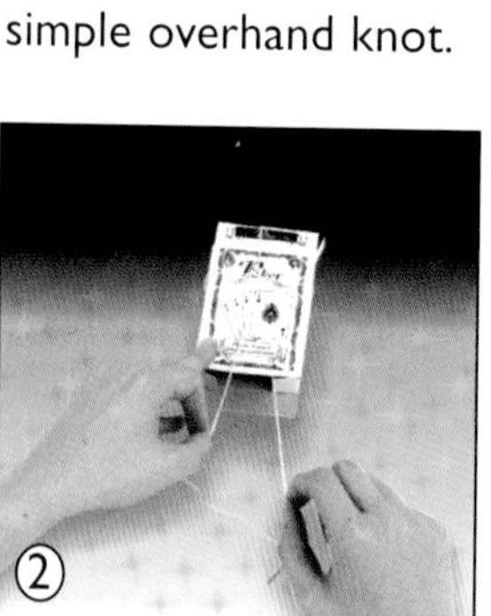

2. Push one end of the string into the box and pull it through to the other side.

3. As you do this, slide the knot off the tube at the same end and push it into the open end. Keep hold of the unthreaded string.

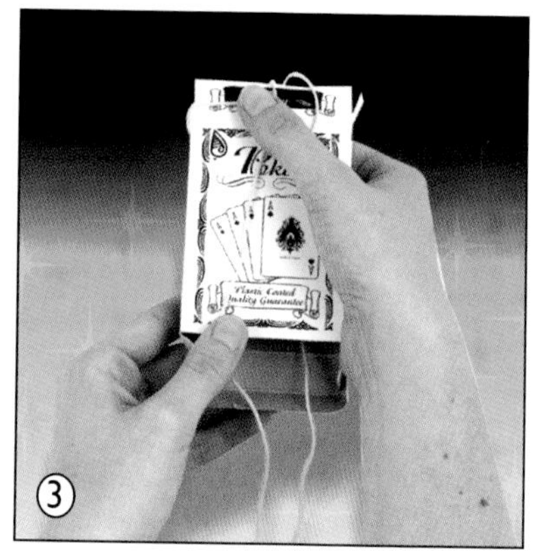

4. As you pull the string through the box, the knot vanishes!

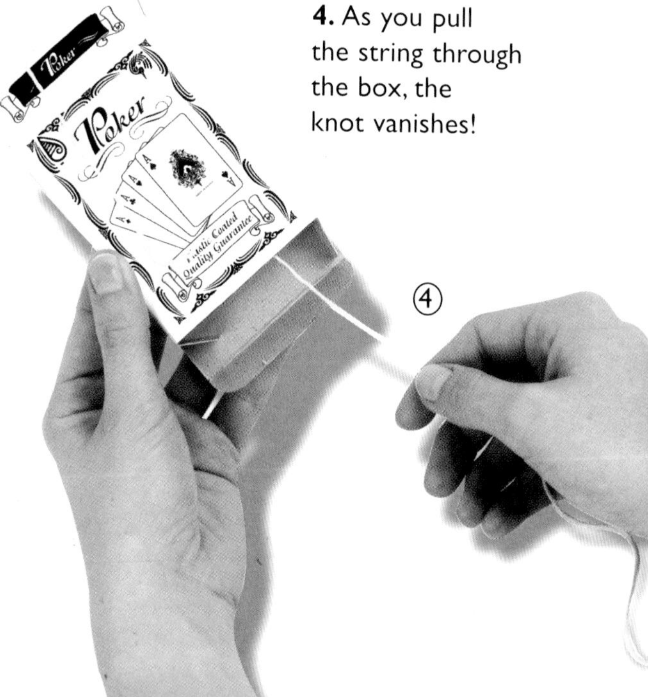

Mind Reading

Baffle your audience by reading someone's mind—but it's all really down to some tricky sleight of hand.

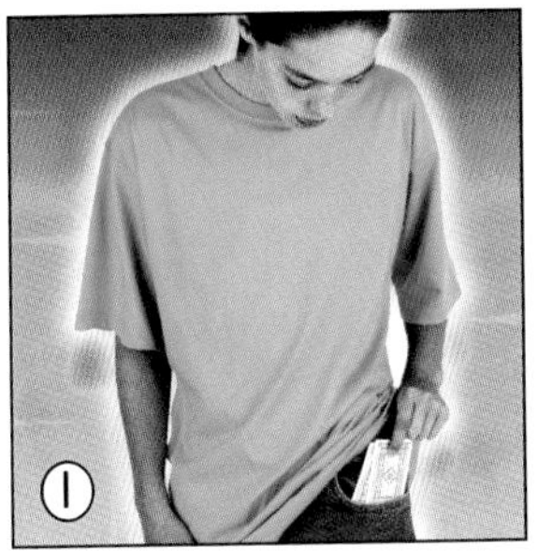

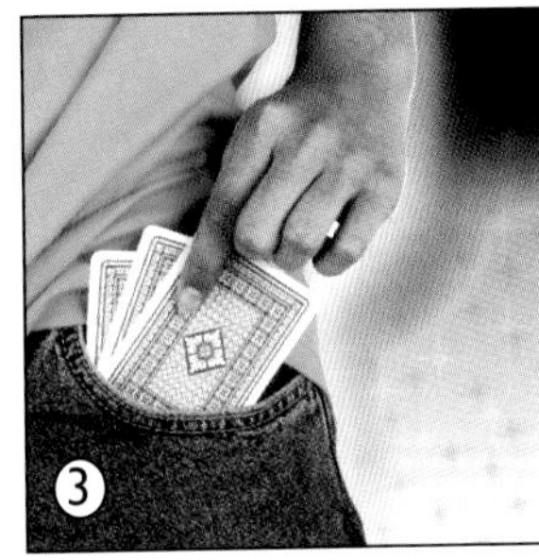

1. Before you begin this trick, put any two cards into your trouser pocket.

2. Ask a member of your audience to shuffle a deck of cards. Deal the top three cards face up on the table.

3. Look at the three cards and memorize them. Then ask your volunteer to think of one of the cards on the table, but not to tell anyone. Pick up the cards, remembering the order they are in, and carefully put them on top of the other two cards already in your pocket.

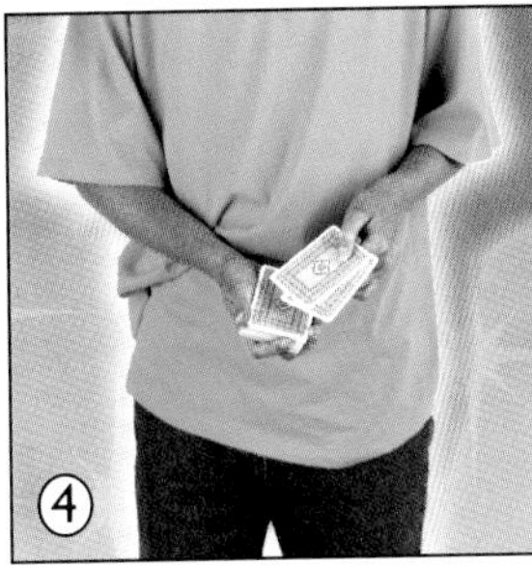

4. Tell your audience that you know which card your volunteer is thinking of. Take out the two cards which you hid in your pocket before you began the trick—the audience will think that you only have one card left in your pocket, but you know you still have three. Return these two cards to the deck without showing their faces.

5. Ask your volunteer to name their card. Reach into your pocket, and because you memorized the order that you put the cards in, you are able to pull out the chosen card with a flourish. Your audience will think that you are an amazing mind reader!

Abracadabra!

A magic spell locates a chosen card!

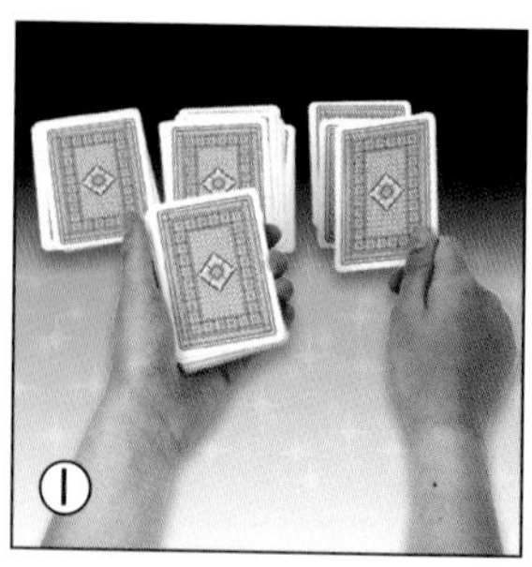

1. Deal three piles of cards, face down, until you have seven in each pile. Set aside the rest of the deck.

2. Ask someone to pick one of the piles.

3. Display the chosen cards in a fan to your volunteer. Ask your volunteer to choose a card, but not to tell you what it is.

Pro Tip

This trick only works if you deal three piles at a time, instead of dealing one pile of seven followed by another two piles of seven.

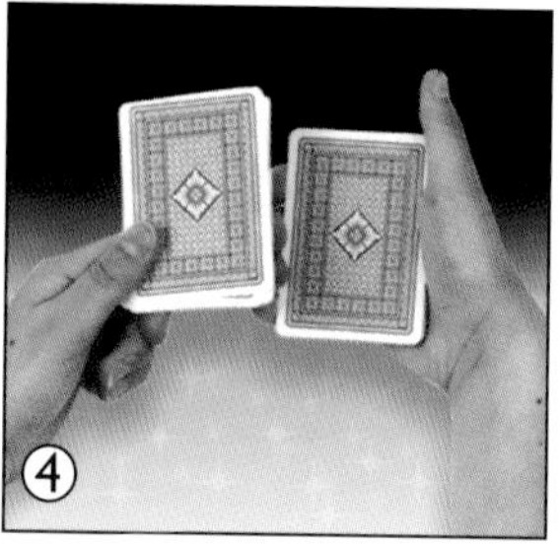

4. Gather up the cards and put the pile containing the chosen card in between the other two piles. Deal the cards in the same way again into three piles of seven.

5. Pick up one pile at a time and display them to the volunteer, asking them to identify the pile which contains their chosen card.

6. Once again, put this pile between the other two and deal out the cards into three piles.

7. Fan out the cards for a third time: ask the volunteer to identify the pile containing their card, then put this pile between the other two.

8. Solemnly spell out the word ABRACADABRA, dealing one card for each of the letters spoken out load. Turn over the final card to show it is the chosen one!

⑧

Magic Shuffle

Magically deal a line of cards in perfect order!

1. You need ten cards for this trick. Arrange them in advance into: eight, three, five, ace, nine, ten, four, six, seven, two.

2. Announce you are going to perform a magic shuffle. Hold up the cards and show them to be in a "random" order.

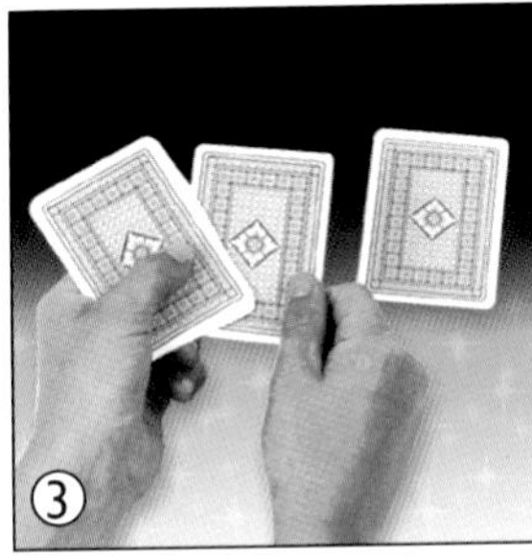

3. Put the first card face down on the table. Put the second card at the bottom of the deck in your hand.

4. Put the third card on top of the one on the table; the fourth at the bottom of the deck. Continue until all the cards are on the table.

5. Pick up the deck and glance through it with dismay. The trick hasn't worked! You forgot to say the magic words.

6. Perform the same shuffle again, but this time saying some magic words.

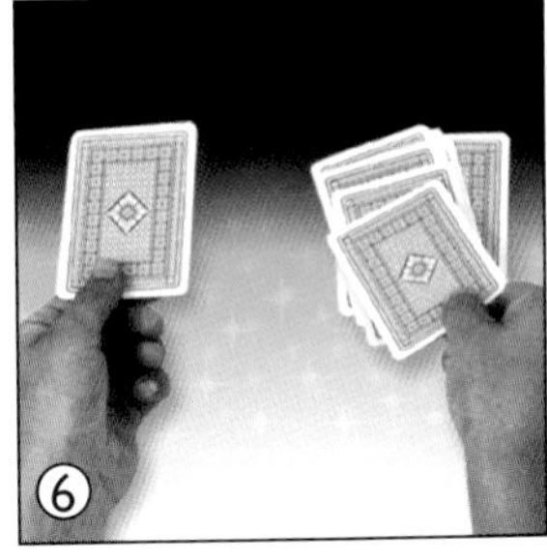

7. Now deal the cards face up in a line on the table: they will be in perfect order.

The Chosen Card

A card chosen by a member of your audience is lost in the deck, but you can still find it!

1. Ask a member of your audience to shuffle a deck of cards. Now take the deck and ask them to select a card and to show the card they have chosen to the rest of the audience.

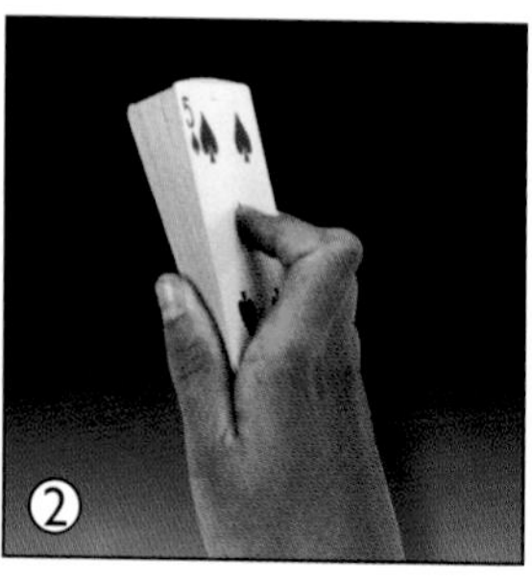

2. While they are doing this, quickly and secretly look at the card which is on the bottom of the deck.

3. Now divide the deck into two. Put the top half of the cards into your left hand. Ask the member of the audience to replace their chosen card on top of this half, then put the remaining cards on top of it.

4. The chosen card will now be below the card that you looked at. To make your trick even more convincing, cut the cards again.

5. Spread the deck of cards face up on a magic table. The card chosen by the member of your audience will be on top of the card which was on the bottom of the deck in step 2.

The Ninth Card

Mystify your audience simply by counting!

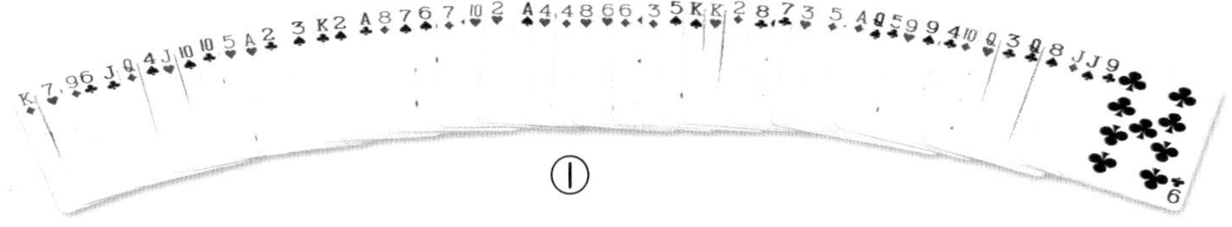

1. Ask a volunteer to shuffle the cards. When they are returned to you, spread the cards with their faces up. Remember the ninth card from the left of the deck. For this example it is the ten of spades.

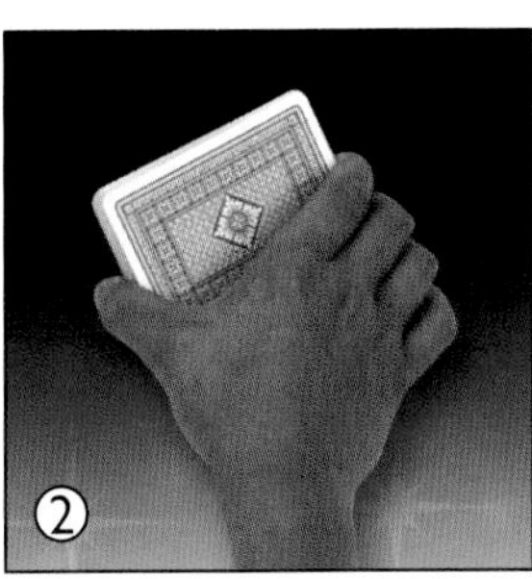

2. Now put the cards into a pile and pick them up.

3. Ask a volunteer to give you a number between 11 and 18. Then count that number of cards off from the top of the deck one at a time, and place them to one side.

4. Say that you will add the two digits of the number you were given together

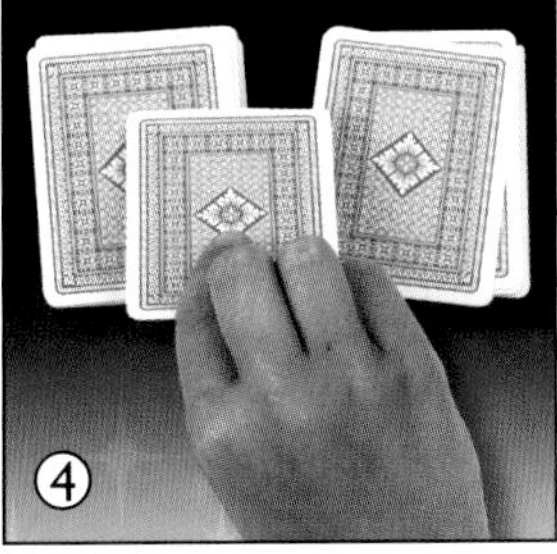

(e.g. if the chosen number was 16, the 1 and 6 added together would give you 7). Then remove that number of cards, one by one, from the top of the smaller pile and put them on top of the bigger pile.

5. Now say that you think the next card will be the ten of spades. Ask a volunteer to turn the next card over. Once again, your audience will be stunned!

Pro Tip

This trick will only work if your volunteer chooses a number between 11 and 18.

Team Game

Before starting this trick, you will need to know the top card of the deck.

1. Shuffle the cards in the way described on page 11.

2. With the cards on your outstretched palm, divide the cards into two piles and balance the top half on your fingers.

③

②

3. Ask a volunteer to look at the top card of the pile nearest them while you look at the top card of the other half.

4. Now place your pile on top of their pile (the one on your fingers). Pretend to announce the card you looked at but in fact name the partner of the card you remembered earlier—so if the card was the three of hearts you say "Three of diamonds." Everyone will be amazed when the volunteer announces the card they saw (in this example it will be the three of hearts).

④

Five-Way Split

This trick uses a more complicated method to find a chosen card.

1. Preparation is the key to the success of this trick. Before you start, take all the diamonds from your deck of cards. Count out a pile of 35 cards—put five diamonds underneath the pile and five on top.

2. Give the deck of cards to a member of the audience, and ask them to deal the cards into five piles, face down on the table. Ask them to pick a card from the middle of one of the piles and to remember that card.

3. Tell your volunteer to put the card face down on top of any of the piles, then ask them to put the piles together to make one deck of cards. Cut the deck several times to make sure their card is well mixed with the others.

4. Spread the deck of cards. To find the right card, scan slowly over the cards. The chosen card will be between two diamonds, so as soon as you see a card splitting two diamonds, you know you have found the right one.

Mind Reading in a Box

Find four chosen cards from the deck without looking!

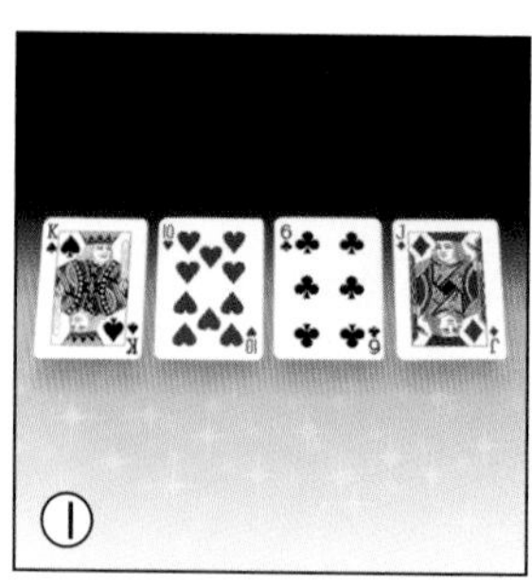
①

③

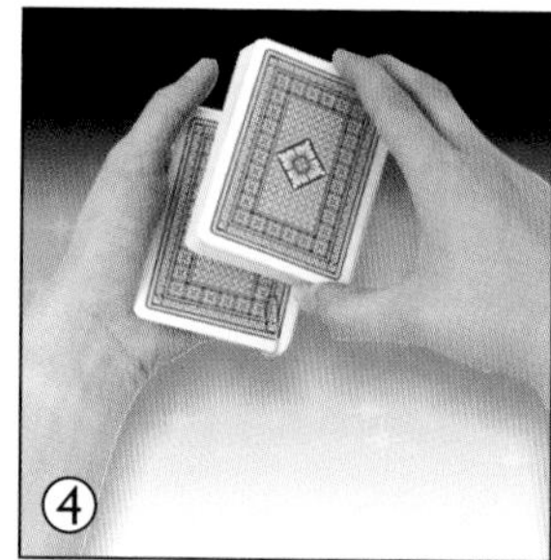
④

1. Before you start, put a paper clip in your pocket. Then ask your volunteer to shuffle the deck, and then select four cards, which they should remember.

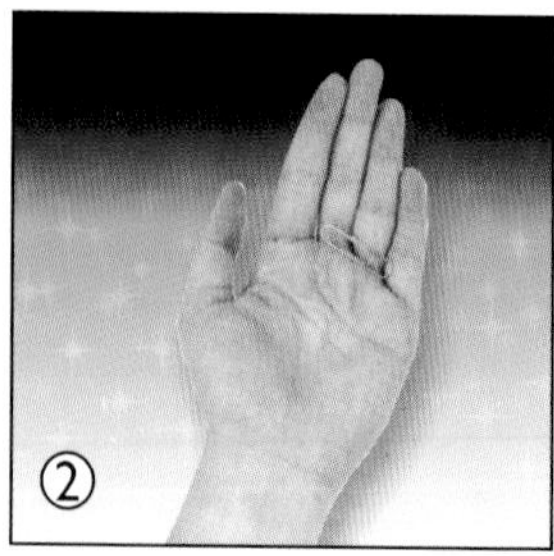
②

2. While they are selecting the cards, secretly take the paper clip out of your pocket and hide it in your left hand.

3. Take the four chosen cards from your audience one at a time, and place them in a fan in your left hand. Secretly slide the bottom of each card into the paper clip, which is hidden by your left thumb.

4. Close up the fan of cards. Take the rest of the deck from your audience and place the fan on top of the deck. Shuffle the cards to mix them up, treating the four cards in the paper clip as one. Make sure that the paper clip is hidden by keeping it towards your body.

5. Put all of your cards into a box—or even a top hat if you have one!—and give it a shake. Your audience will think that all of the cards are being mixed together, but you know that the chosen cards are being held together by a paper clip.

6. Say some magical words, then reach into the box and find the four cards. Remove the paper clip, leaving it in the box. Then show that you have found their selected cards!

Pro Tip

When you shuffle the cards, why not tell a joke to the audience to divert their attention from what you are doing.

Back to Back

The key to this trick is to do it quickly. That way, you'll be sure to fool your audience.

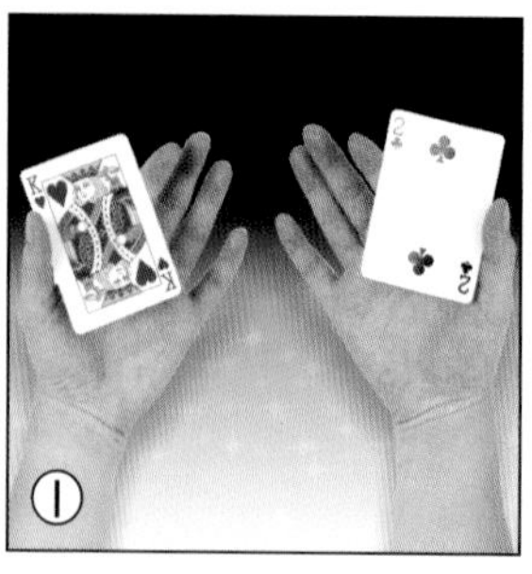

1. Hold a card in each hand by its side between your thumb and first finger—the faces should be directly opposite each other. Now position your hands about twelve inches apart.

2. Slowly bring your hands together until each card can be gripped by the thumb and second finger of the opposite hand. There should be a small gap of about half an inch between the cards.

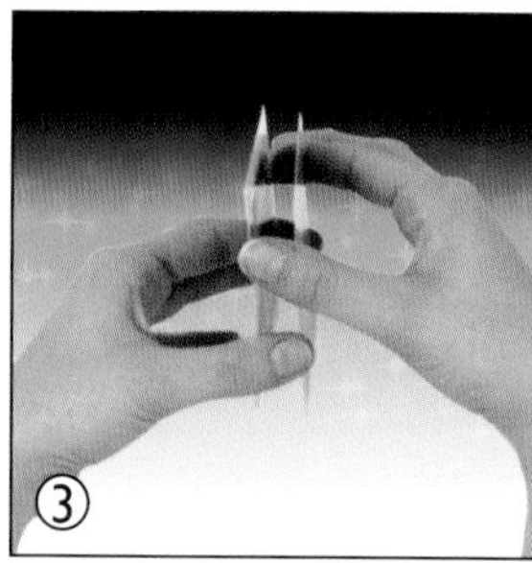

3. Raise the cards towards your mouth and tell your audience that you will blow between them and they will magically change places.

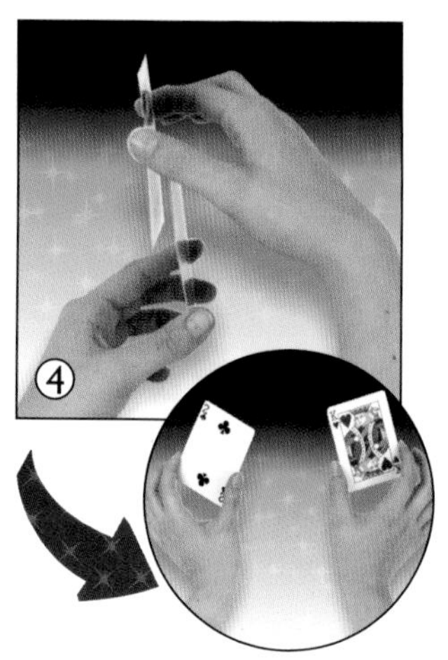

4. As soon as you have blown between the cards, start to move your hands back to their original positions twelve inches apart, the right hand taking the left card, the left hand taking the right card.

Pro Tip

This trick needs a lot of practice before you perform it. Start slowly and gradually build up speed until you can make the change without hesitation—it is the smoothness of your move that will fool your audience.

In the Picture

This trick is so good, have a camera handy to take a picture of your volunteer's face when you've fooled them once again.

1. You'll need two decks of cards for this trick. First, decide which card you are going to force. Let's say, for this example it's the seven of spades.

2. Hide the duplicate of the card you are going to force under a chair, or even a bucket—any hiding place will do.

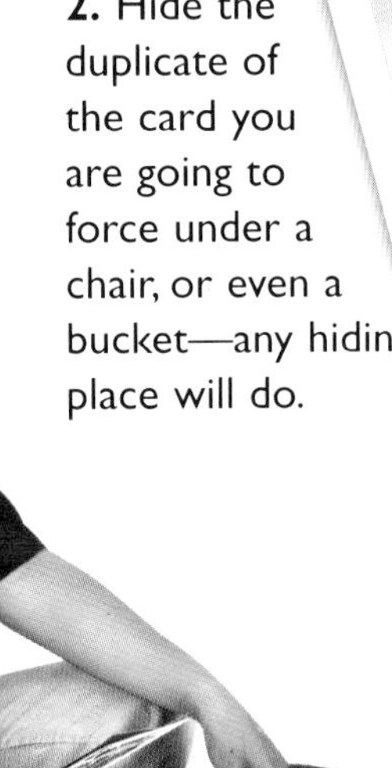

3. Take the deck of cards and "force" (see page 8) your volunteer to choose the card that is hidden.

4. When the card has been chosen, ask your volunteer to look under the bucket. They will be bewildered when they see that the card is the same as the one they chose!

④

Mega Mind Reading

What's better than reading one person's mind? Reading two, of course!

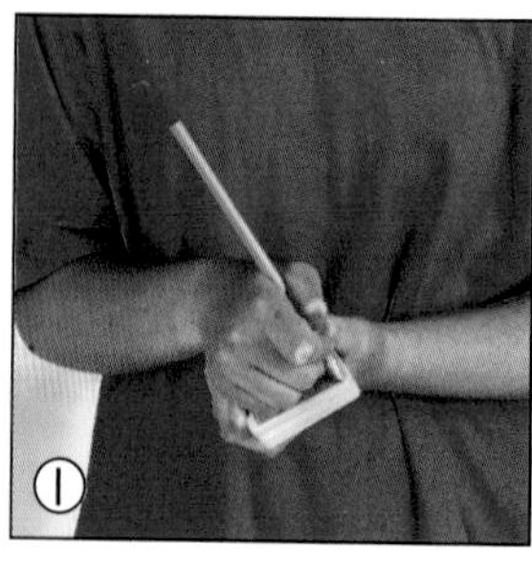
①

1. Prepare your trick. Take any card, and on its back put one pencil dot in the top left-hand and bottom right-hand corners. Put this card in your pocket until you are ready to use it.

2. Shuffle the deck of cards, then ask two volunteers to select a card each, which they need to remember without telling anyone.

3. While they are remembering their cards, secretly retrieve the marked card from your pocket and put it on the bottom of the deck.

4. Ask one of your volunteers to replace their card on top of the deck. Cut the deck. Place the top half of the cards in your left hand, then put the other half on top. The marked card is now on top of the first chosen card.

5. Spread the deck face down to find your marked card. Cut the deck in half one card below the marked card, then put the top half of cards underneath the other half. This takes the first chosen card to the bottom of the deck, with the marked card above it. Quickly look at the bottom card and remember it.

6. Ask your second volunteer to replace their card on the top of the deck. Cut the deck as you did in step 4 to bring the first and second chosen cards and the marked card together.

7. Announce to your audience that you will now read your first volunteer's mind! Make a big show of

②

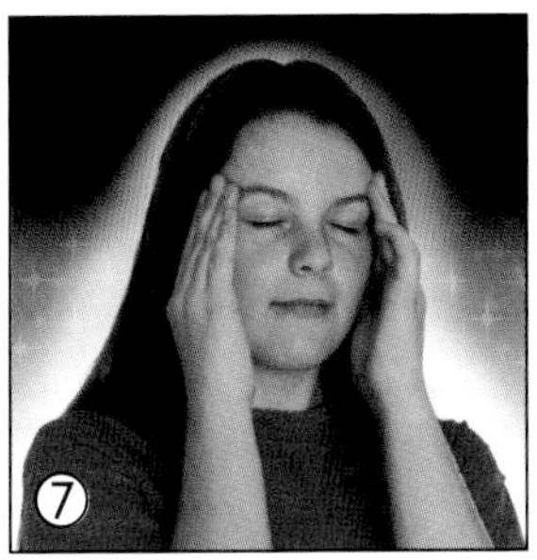

concentrating hard, closing your eyes and breathing deeply. Then reveal the name of the chosen card (which you found in step 5), ask your volunteer to confirm that this is the right one, and your audience will gasp.

8. They will be even more amazed when you complete the trick and read a second person's mind. To do this, spread the deck of cards in front of you. The second chosen card will be on top of the first chosen card. Of course, now that you know the secret of how to read two minds at once, there's no reason why you can't read three, four or even five!

Flipper

A chosen card finds itself by turning in mid air!

1. Find a chosen card (see page 32). Tell your audience that you are going to make the chosen card flip itself over, and while you are doing this, secretly cut the card to the top of the deck.

2. Holding the deck in your left hand, bring your right hand over the cards. While you are doing this, push the top card slightly to the right with your left thumb.

3. With your right hand, lift the deck up, then throw it straight down into your left hand.

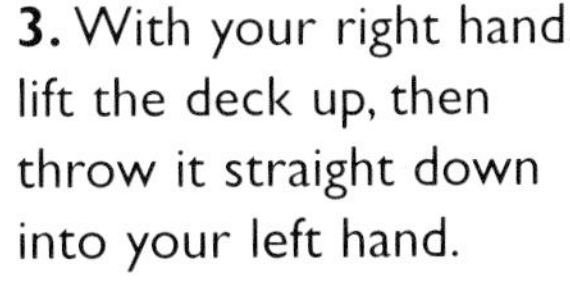

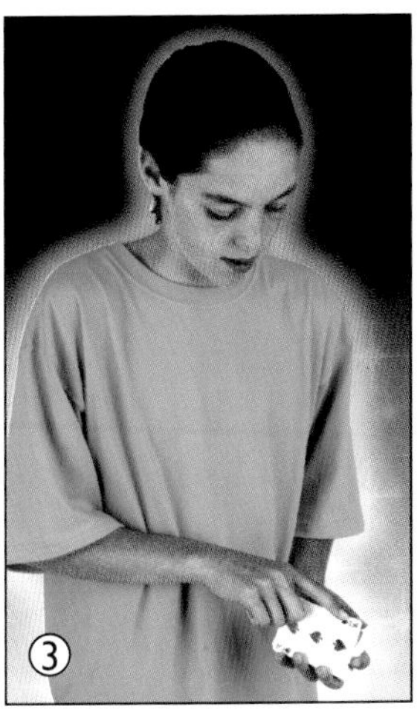

4

4. Your audience will be amazed as the chosen card flips over in mid air, and then lands on top of the deck!

52-Card Scatter

This is a spectacular way to find a chosen card—but it takes nerve!

1. You need to start by losing and then finding a chosen card (see page 32). Secretly cut the card to the top of the deck.

②

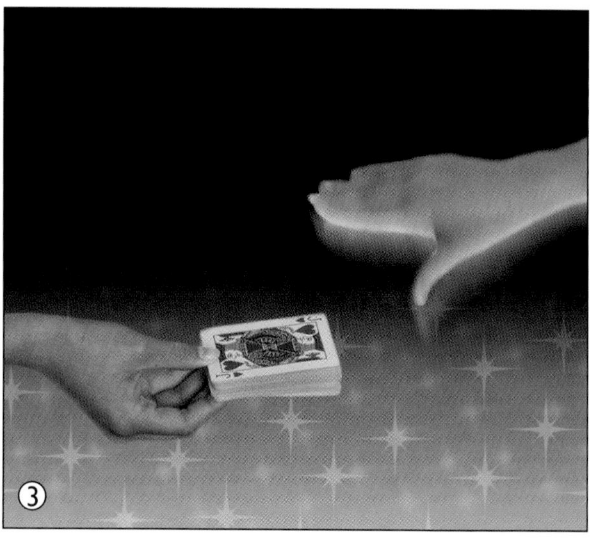

③

2. Now ask a member of your audience to hold their hand out, palm upwards. Then position the deck face up in their hand, so that their fingers stretch underneath the cards for at least one inch and their thumb is on the top of the deck for about half an inch. Ask them to hold the deck firmly.

3. Hold your nerve with this step! Strike down with your hand on the end of the deck which is not being held.

4. All the cards will scatter to the floor, except the chosen card, which is being held firmly between the fingers and thumb of your volunteer.

3a

4

Magic Spell

The secret to this trick is to spell it out!

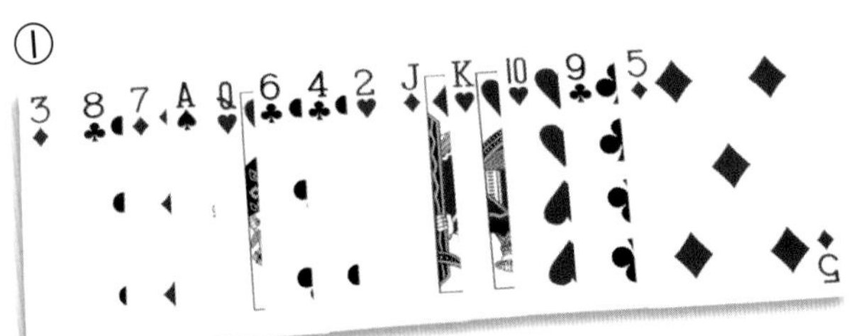
①

④

1. Before you start the trick, remove and arrange thirteen cards as follows: three, eight, seven, ace, queen, six, four, two, jack, king, ten, nine and five. Put these on top of the deck.

③

②

2. Shuffle the cards but make sure the thirteen cards from step 1 remain at the top of the deck.

3. Take the thirteen cards from the top and spread them in a fan face down.

4. Now, here comes the tricky bit. Spell out the word "ace" and, as you do this, remove one card from the top of the deck for each letter and place it on the bottom. Then turn over the fourth card—it will be the ace!

5. Do the same for each card. You must do it in the order ace, two, three, four, five, six, seven, eight, nine, ten, jack, queen, king for the trick to work.

⑤
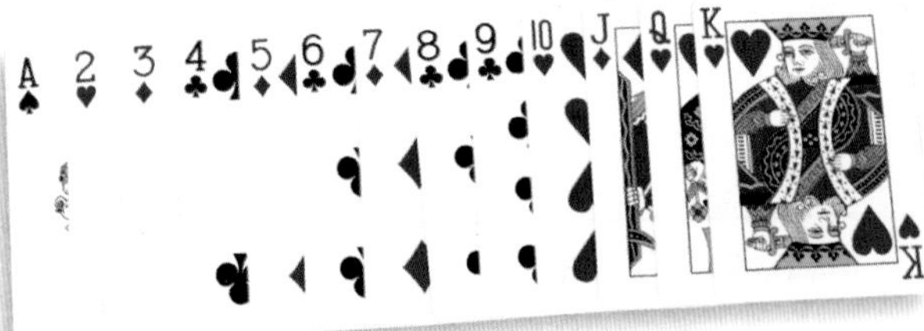

Aces High

Play a trick without even touching the cards.

1. Before performing the trick, place the four aces on top of the deck.

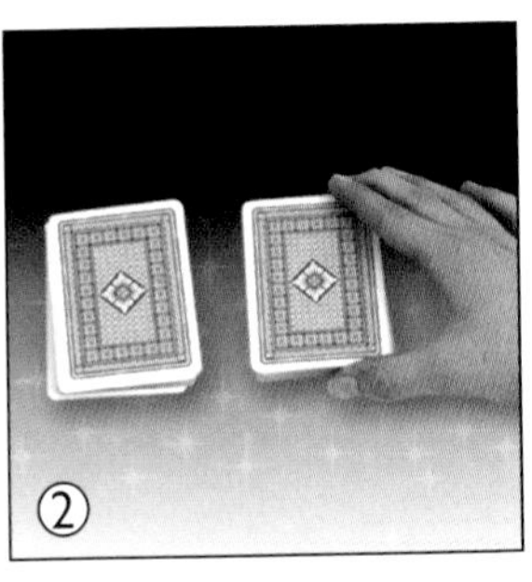

2. Ask a volunteer to cut the deck into two piles. Keep track of which pile the aces are on.

3. Now ask the volunteer to cut the two piles into two more piles so you now have four piles. The aces should be on one of the end piles.

4. Ask your volunteer to take three cards from the pile furthest away from the pile containing the aces. The volunteer should then put these cards at the bottom of the pile. Then ask them to deal the top three cards, one at a time, onto each of the other three piles.

5. The volunteer should then do the same with the other three piles in sequence. But, make sure that the last pile to be dealt with is the one containing the aces.

6. Now when you turn over the top card of each pile the four aces will be revealed.

Pointing Exercise

You'll need to use your thumb for this sleight of hand!

1. Ask a volunteer to shuffle a deck of cards and then remove a few.

②

③

2. Take the chosen cards and fan them out so that they are facing towards another volunteer. Ask the second volunteer to point at a card.

3. Even though you can't see the faces of the cards you will know the identity of the card chosen. This is because you use your left thumb to push up the bottom corner of the card so you can see the index.

4. Announce the card your volunteer has chosen. They will be astounded by your mind-reading power.

④

Back to Front

Before performing this trick, place the six of any suit face up in the sixth position from the bottom of the deck.

1. Ask a volunteer to pick a card from your fan and remember it. When you are doing this, make sure that you don't expose the reversed card.

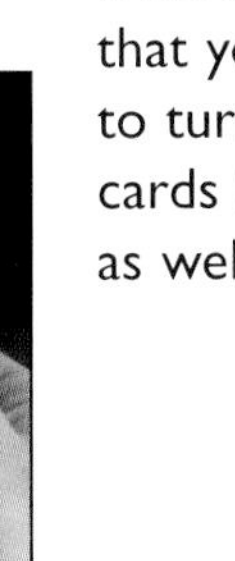

2. Your volunteer should now place the chosen card on the bottom of the deck.

3. Cut the deck a few times, until the card is somewhere in the middle of the deck.

4. Announce that this trick is too easy and that you have decided to turn one of the cards in the deck over as well as finding your volunteer's card. Spread the cards face down across the table until the reversed card becomes visible. Then turn over the sixth card to the left of the six. This will be your volunteer's card.

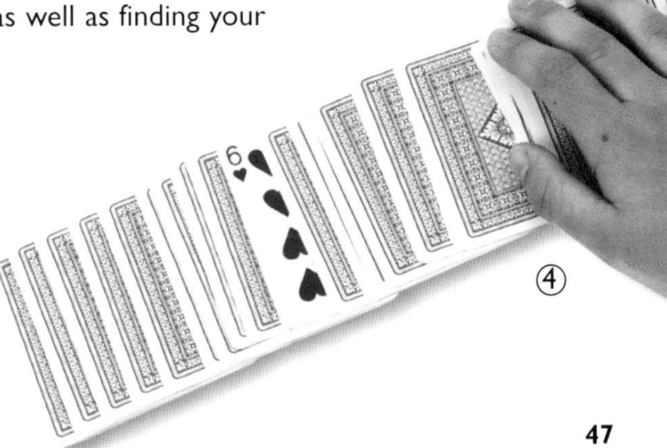

Glossary

Here you will find explanations for terms in the book that you may not be familiar with, and also some other terms that you might come across while using playing cards.

Ace any of the four playing cards with only one spot.

Cut dividing the deck into two random parts after shuffling.

Deck another name for the pack of playing cards.

Fan the shape in which dealt cards are usually held in the hand or the shape in which they are usually placed on the table.

Index the symbol in the corner that shows which card it is.

Force tricking someone into picking the card you want them to without them realizing.

Joker a card that does not belong to any suit, nor does it have a number. It can be used in some games and tricks but is not always required.

Overhand shuffle a basic shuffle.

Patter talking in order to distract your audience from what you are doing.

Royal any of the jacks, queens or kings.

Shuffle mixing up the deck in order to change the order of the cards.

Suit any of the four sets of thirteen cards: clubs, diamonds, hearts or spades.